D1569546

TEARS ON THE CHURCH HOUSE FLOOR

DAN PRATT

WESTBOW
PRESS®
A DIVISION OF THOMAS NELSON
& ZONDERVAN

WestBow Press books may be ordered through booksellers or by contacting:

WestBow Press
A Division of Thomas Nelson & Zondervan
1663 Liberty Drive
Bloomington, IN 47403
www.westbowpress.com
1 (866) 928-1240

ISBN: 978-1-9736-2303-8 (sc)
ISBN: 978-1-9736-2304-5 (hc)
ISBN: 978-1-9736-2302-1 (e)

Library of Congress Control Number: 2018903187

Print information available on the last page.

WestBow Press rev. date: 03/21/2018

I would like to dedicate this book to Bill Thomas Pratt. He is my grandson. Our relationship in this life was not to be; however eternity awaits us. Bill Thomas save me a seat next to Jesus at the feast.

Love Papa

CONTENTS

CONTENTS

ACKNOWLEDGEMENT

This book was made possible by the tireless efforts of my editor and daughter-in-law Celeste Rose Pratt. Like a fine silver smith she drew off the dross to increase the clarity of the message.

Seth Deitch's illustrations breathed life into the stories. He is gifted.

I would also like to acknowledge the Mountains Climbers Bible class at the Oak Hills Church in San Antonio, Texas for their unshakeable faith which has supplied me with a constant source of inspiration. Jesus spoke of them when he called on his followers to be salt and light in this world.

FOREWORD

Come with me to a special place. Journey with me to a world of waxwings, old black dogs and wooden frame houses. Let's visit the land of loud laughter, tender prayers and heartfelt tears. You need to know Ol' Bill, a hound named Sister and the Mountain Climbers. Take a moment and travel into the land of a good man, my good friend, Dan Pratt.

If you've never met him, I hope you get to do so. His handshake is warm and greeting is genuine. He's a composite of story-teller and engineer, Tennessee and Texas, church elder and fisherman, Bible School teacher and world traveler and country boy. He's full of joy, not because of a pain-free life, but because life's bruises have made him better. He speaks with a wisdom that emerges from a trail well-traveled.

He's done you and me a favor. He's captured snapshots of his story in a book. We have a chance to read it and learn. I've done so. I'm hoping you will do the same.

Max Lucado
Minister and Author

INTRODUCTION

Pass me not, O gentle savior,
Hear my humble cry;
While on others thou art calling,
Do not pass me by.
—Fanny J. Crosby

As Jesus left the Mount of Transfiguration and set his face toward Jerusalem, he knew the cross was waiting for him there. He told his disciples exactly what would unfold, and yet along the journey to Jerusalem, James and John could only make requests to have special positions in the coming new order. How often do we hear Jesus's words plainly spoken, only to come up with our own agenda and plans?

As the journey continued, Jesus and the disciples passed through Jericho and encountered a blind beggar named Bartimaeus sitting at his usual place on the roadway out of town. Bartimaeus was alone and majorly disabled and had experienced disappointment after disappointment as he looked for hope, a coin, or a simple kind word from the travelers on their way out of town.

Bartimaeus heard the crowd approaching and learned that it was Jesus passing by. While he could not see, Bartimaeus was keenly aware of Jesus since he had heard every casual word spoken on the street of the miracles performed and hoped that this day might be different for him if he could only get the attention of the one called Jesus.

Are we not just like Bartimaeus? We try to get God's attention, hoping that he might turn our way and send us some relief for life's burdens. I see us as blind like Bartimaeus in that we cannot see what God is doing until we see what He has done. What we cannot see in our blindness is that our God does not pass us by and instead already has the forces of heaven at work to minister to our hurts.

This book is a deeply personal story about grief that our family passed through in the span of exactly one year. We lost a grandson, a mother, and a pet. It is also a story about our incredible God who did not just stop and turn our way but rather wove himself into our lives over a fifty-year span to prepare us for this exact season of grief. This book's goal is to show you how your tears matter to God. He values you and will not leave you alone in your sorrows. Like Bartimaeus, there is coming a day when we will see clearly all that God has done in our lives.

The nails of the cross awaited Jesus in Jerusalem, but he stopped to heal a blind man who called out in desperation to him. That day marked the beginning of the rest of the story for Bartimaeus. My deepest prayer is for you to read this book and allow God to show you *your* rest of the story.

TEARS ON THE CHURCH FLOOR

Record my lament;
List my tears on your scroll
Are they not in your record?
—Psalm 56:8 (NIV)

At Oak Hills Church, we close each worship time with an offer to all who would like intercessory prayer. As the service comes to a close, the elders and their wives go to the front and back of the auditorium to pray with those who respond.

This was a special Sunday morning because it was the last service we were holding in our gymnasium-style auditorium. The auditorium had roll-up bleachers and removable chairs, with a light-gray concrete floor. Our maintenance crew could convert the space from worship center to gym in a few hours. There had been countless prayers that had risen to heaven from this space over the years. The next week we would be having our worship service in our new space, which was a more traditional church auditorium with carpet in the front of the auditorium and seats fixed to the floor. As a church, we were excited to be moving into the new space, but there was a sadness that settled on us as well. To the world it was a gym and multiuse space, but to the church, it was where we had communed with God Almighty for many years.

The call for prayer was made, so Nancy and I went to the front of the auditorium to pray with any who would come. One

1

woman stepped into the aisle with a downcast look on her face. Her movements were measured and slow, as if life had drained away her joy.

Nancy and I collected her details so we might know how to pray. She was a mother whose adult son had lost his way. The three of us formed a triangle by placing our arms around each other's shoulders and bowing our heads toward the center of the triangle. We invited God to join us, making it a holy triangle. We started the prayer by recognizing this mother's faith and affirming ours. The writer of the Hebrew letter states, "Without faith it is impossible to please God because anyone that would come to him must believe that he exists and that he rewards those who earnestly seek him" (Hebrews 11:6 NIV). Faith always draws the full attention of heaven. All the angels grow quiet when the earnest heart comes into the throne room of God. There is a hush that sweeps the room as the earnest heart expresses its desperation, and with the expression of desperation, tears often flow.

We finished our prayer and hugged tightly. As our triangle broke up, the shadows moved away, and I could see her tears on the church house floor. *Dear desperate and heartbroken child of God, know that every one of those tears is recorded in heaven.*

I had set time aside to work on this story. It was a rainy afternoon, so my excuses were limited. Nancy declared, "It is a rainy afternoon—let's go to a movie." *The Shack* had just opened. I put up a weak argument and soon found myself standing in line for two tickets to see *The Shack*. The film is a work of fiction (written by William Paul Young) that deals with a father coming to grips with deep pain in his life by spending the weekend with the Holy Trinity. There was a scene in the movie that I needed to see to write this story.

Mack is the main character of the movie. He and his wife, Nan, have three children: Josh, Kate, and Missy. Mack's relationship with God is wide while Nan's relationship is deep. One weekend

Nan attends a God-centered conference, so Mack and the kids go camping.

Near the end of the camping trip, Josh and Kate are canoeing and Missy is coloring a picture of a princess at the picnic table outside their camper. Mack is busy breaking down the camp and consulting with Missy about her work of art. To gain her father's attention, Kate stands up in the canoe and waves at her father, causing the canoe to tip over. Mack races to the dock and dives in the lake to save his son, Josh, from drowning.

During all the commotion, another worst nightmare for a parent occurs: a child predator grabs Missy, and her body is later discovered in a mountain shack. Mack has the unthinkable task of going to that shack to identify his precious daughter's body. Sometime later, Mack receives a cruel note in his mailbox that reads, "It's been a while. I've missed you. I'll be at the shack next weekend if you want to get together." It is signed "Papa." Mack gets a sick feeling and thinks, *Could this be the monster that took our Missy away?*

Mack goes to the shack with gun in hand, thinking that he will encounter the murderer. Instead he encounters a stranger dressed as a laborer who leads him to a cottage set in the midst of paradise. Inside the cottage, he meets God the Father (Papa), God the Son (Jesus), and God the Holy Spirit (Sarayu). Papa is a large African American woman. Jesus has a Middle Eastern look and is dressed as a carpenter. Sarayu is a beautiful Asian woman. She has a warm glow about her. Her hair appears to be floating on a breeze even though the air inside the cottage is still.

Papa warmly accepts Mack. She smells of his mother's perfume and tells him of her deep love for him. With his emotions in overdrive, tears begin to form in Mack's eyes. Sarayu steps forward from behind Papa. Her finger runs across Mack's lower eyelid to collect his tears, and she deposits them in a crystal vial. As she places the top on the vial she looks at Mack and says, "We collect that which we value."

3

Your tears matter to God. Did you know that God collects them? He has always been in the tear-collection business. Even before the days of Naomi and Ruth, God has been collecting the tears of his children. The story of Naomi and Ruth is found in the book of Ruth in the Bible. It has only four chapters but tells a story of the rich relationship that bonded these two women.

In the days when the judges ruled Israel, there was a famine that came up on the land. In a desperate move to avoid starving, Elimelech decided to take his wife, Naomi, and their two sons to live in the land of Moab. The harshness of the times and the separation from the familiar surroundings of their small village of Bethlehem caused tears to flow from Naomi's sad eyes. The times were hard, but she remained secure in her husband, Elimelech, and in the hope for a new start in Moab.

Life in Moab produced deep sorrow when Elimelech died and left Naomi with her two sons. The sons married Moabite women named Orpah and Ruth. Ten years passed, and both sons died. Naomi had now made three trips to the graveyard: first as a widow, and on the second and third trips, she returns childless. In your mind, position yourself as an unseen observer in the home of Naomi. She returns home from her third trip to the graveyard and closes the door. There is thick silence that rings in her ears and a pain of grief aching in her heart. She is crushed in spirit by her loss. She sits at the kitchen table with no appetite and only tears for food.

My sister Jane knows the heart of Naomi; her husband Jerold died in his sleep at only sixty-four. Jerold had retired two years earlier. He was a successful businessman who was loved by his church and by the town of Bowling Green, Kentucky, and his untimely passing was a shock to all. When the door first closed and Jane was by herself, the weeping was continuous. After a year had passed, Jane told me she only allowed herself to cry one time each day. The tears of a widow do not go unnoticed by God. The book of James tells us that if you want to be close to the heart of God, get close to the heart of the widow (James 1:27 NIV).

Naomi's grief was compounded by the loss of her livelihood. When what little wealth Elimelech might have left Naomi was gone, poverty became the most pressing issue. Naomi hears that the times have turned for the better back at home, so she decides to return to Judah with her two daughters-in-law.

Three widows are on the road to Judah. They are traveling not to visit family and friends but rather to survive. Along the route, Naomi appeals to her daughters-in-law to return to the security of their mother's home. Orpah sees the wisdom in that advice and leaves for home. But Ruth cannot tear herself away from her mother-in-law and makes one of the most tender statements of commitment in the Bible, saying, "Don't urge me to leave you, or to turn back from you. Where you go I will go, and where you stay I will stay. Your people will be my people and your God my God. Where you die I will die, and there I will be buried. May the Lord deal with me, be it ever so severely, if anything but death separates you and me" (Ruth 1:16–17 NIV). Naomi was truly loved by Ruth.

Naomi and Ruth travel the dusty road to Bethlehem, not knowing what the future holds and lamenting over the past. When they arrive at the city gate, some of the women of Bethlehem recognize Naomi. They exclaim, "Could this be Naomi?" Naomi responds, "Don't call me Naomi, but call me Mara because the Almighty has made my life very bitter. I went away full but the Lord has brought me back empty. Why call me Naomi? The Lord has afflicted me; the Almighty has brought misfortune upon me" (Ruth 1:20–21 NIV).

The name *Naomi* means one filled with joy while *Mara* means one filled with bitterness. We started this story with a woman shedding tears on the church house floor because her joy-filled life had become bitter. Her expectations of a prosperous life for her bouncing baby boy were snatched away by the devil's brew. In a sense we all have traveled the road that Naomi and this brokenhearted Texas mama traveled. Our loss may not have been as severe, but our expectations were crushed, leaving us angry and perhaps bitter.

Do you want a good, life-size example of what to do to turn things around? The Bible states that we should not let the sun go down on our anger (Ephesians 4:26 NIV). If the sun sets on an angry spirit within us, then the devil has gained an advantage. Life may not have turned out the way we had hoped, but we are not without hope. Want to stop the devil in his tracks? Do you want to do it right now? If you do, then follow the example of the Texas mama. Step out into the aisle of faith and pray to God. If you want to add some more horsepower to the appeal, then find a friend and form a holy triangle, inviting God to join. Heaven will grow quiet as a peace that surpasses understanding is dispatched to help you work through the tears.

Our story began with the last service in the Oak Hills gym-style sanctuary. A Texas mama demonstrated her faith by appealing to God through intercessory prayer. Her tears on the church house floor inspired the title for this book. We would move to the new traditional sanctuary the next week, which was designed with theater-style seats that would be firmly anchored to the concrete floor. There were twenty-six hundred seats in the new auditorium, and each seat was covered in plastic. Someone had a great idea concerning opening the new sanctuary: We would call our prayer team members to pray over each seat, and after the prayer, the plastic cover would be removed.

The auditorium was still under construction, so we had to schedule times for the prayer team members to pray so the construction folks could step aside during prayer sessions. My work calls me out of town each week, so it was difficult for me to make the appointed times, but I wanted to be part of this prayer effort, so I made arrangements to get back to San Antonio for the last prayer time slot. When I entered the auditorium, it was overwhelming to see almost all of the plastic covers removed. For over two hours, I was privileged to pray over the chairs on the church house floor. As I prayed, the tears fell onto the dusty plastic and rolled back the dust as they made their way to the floor. I thought to myself, *When I am dead and gone, there will be hurting people who will wet the church house floor from this chair.*

Dear child of God, do not be bitter. Be a Naomi, not a Mara. Your tears matter to God; He collects each tear that falls to the church house floor. Those tears shed in this life are awaiting your arrival in heaven, where there will be no more tears! The apostle John writes in the book of Revelation, "And I heard a loud voice from the throne saying, 'Now the dwelling of God is with men, and he will live with them. They will be his people, and God himself will be with them and be their God. He will wipe away every tear from their eyes. There will be no more death or mourning or crying or pain, for the old order of things has passed away'" (Revelation 21:3–4 NIV).

In thinking about these words from Revelation, I am reminded of the closing lines in a poem I wrote to my sons, Bill and Joshua, encouraging them to follow God and live their lives wisely:

> When this life is o'er
> Across Jordon's stormy banks I will roar
> And set myself on Canaan's shore
> And there in His presence time will be no more.
>
> There is help for today and hope for tomorrow
> when we trust God.
>
> God is our refuge and strength, an ever-present
> help in trouble. Therefore we will not fear, though
> the earth give way and the mountains fall into
> the heart of the sea, though its waters roar and
> foam and the mountains quake with their surging.
> (Psalm 46:1–3 NIV)

THE DUPLEX ON FIFTH AVENUE

Even the sparrow has found a *home*, and the swallow a nest for herself, where she may have her young—a place near your altar, O Lord Almighty, my King and my God. (Psalm 84:3 NIV)

The year was 1962. My sister and I lived with our father and mother in a white frame house on the four-lane highway going into Springfield, Tennessee. The house was a sturdy cottage with windows wrapped around its exterior. At night, those windows glowed with a twinkling, warm light, creating a scene that could have been the subject of a Thomas Kincaid painting.

We lived in the perfect house in a perfect neighborhood consisting of a dozen houses along a dead-end street that was shaped like the crescent moon. James Dean was a crusty old mason who owned a field at the bend in the street. It was covered with fescue and clover that Mr. Dean groomed with his riding lawn mower so we could play baseball. It was the '60s, and there were kids everywhere. They were darting about on bicycles or playing baseball in the afternoons. After dark we would rally at the streetlight in front of Mr. Dean's house and play hide and go seek until our mothers called us in for a bath and bed. The next day we would go from bikes to baseball to bed, in the same order. In the world of a six-year-old, it could not get any better. If Norman Rockwell wanted to paint an all-American neighborhood in the early '60s, he should have positioned his easel on Crescent Drive on a summer afternoon.

The times were unique. The first televised presidential debates came into our living rooms that year. I remember sitting in front of our black-and-white TV to watch John Kennedy and Richard Nixon debate for the presidency of the United States. America was about to elect its youngest and one of its most dynamic presidents. His vision would awaken the creative spirit of America to place a man on the moon. When he laid out the vision, he said that within this decade we would land and safely return a man from the moon. President Kennedy would not live to see it, but in July of 1969, Neil Armstrong made one small step for man and one giant leap for humankind as he stepped on to the surface of the moon.

Our neighborhood was fit for a Rockwell painting, and the American dream seemed to be taking on new life with a visionary president leading our nation forward, but all was not well in our home or America, for the old serpent Satan was on the move sowing seeds of discontent. The '60s would be marked with not one but three assassinations, and the Vietnam War produced a steady stream of flag-draped coffins at Andrews Air Base each week. Riots broke out across the nation protesting the war and the lack of civil rights. Satan always seeks to divide. We watched the divide play out on our televisions each night, but I also watched as our home was under attack.

The neighbors on Crescent Drive could survey our home, and from their perspective, all looked to be in order. We were a typical early '60s family. Mother stayed at home and took care of us. Her house was clean and smelled of Pine Sol. My father and uncles had an animal feed business that fit well into the agricultural backbone of the Robertson County economy. We had one car. It was a 1959 Plymouth that my father bought new.

Things are often not what they appear to be, and this thriving family of the early '60s was one of those cases. Our neighborhood had enough boys in it to field a football team. When I came out to play, I noticed a difference in the way I looked compared to the other boys. They would have the occasional patch on their blue jeans, but my jeans were a tapestry of patches. My only pair of jeans had patches on top of patches. Unfortunately, my father had the ability to make money but not to manage it.

When it came time for me to go to school, there was an argument that broke out between my mother and father concerning my lack of clothes. I knew she won when the next day, Mother led me into my bedroom where on the bed laid two pair of new blue jeans and two new shirts with new socks and a pair of Red Ball Jet tennis shoes.

Those new clothes were an indescribable gift to me. Have you ever in any way felt the spotlight of discrimination shine on you wherever you turn? My patches made me stand out. More than standing out, I felt like a rat turd in a bowl of white rice. Perhaps some might be offended by this crude analogy, but I am here to tell you that the humiliation brought by discrimination is far worse. New clothes were not the indescribable gift, but rather the true gift was the lifting of my shame. New blue jeans made me blend in with the new first-grade class at Chetham Park Elementary School, as they served as a Band-Aid on a cut that needed stiches.

There was a reason for my patchwork jeans and my mother's lack of a decent Sunday coat. My father was under attack from the evil one.

> When tempted, no one should say, "God is tempting me." For God cannot be tempted by evil, nor does he tempt anyone; But each one is tempted when, by his own evil desire, he is dragged away and enticed. Then, after desire has conceived, It gives birth to sin; and sin, When it is full-grown, gives birth to death. (James 1:13–15 NIV)

11

My father was being dragged away and enticed. As Satan's grip became tighter, the emotional state of our family and finances were dragged away as well. My father was attracted to another woman.

Behind the door of the Thomas Kincaid cottage on Crescent Drive, Satan had sowed the seeds of divorce. My parents began to argue and drew apart. My father began to sleep in the front room. One morning, my mother discovered a gift that my father had purchased for the other woman. As you could imagine, a heated argument erupted, and as he raised his hand to strike my mother, I threw my six-year-old frame against his leg in defense of her, thinking I might stop him. Just like a bucket of water thrown on a campfire, the emotions were extinguished immediately by the actions of a son standing up to his own father. In that moment, my father saw the ugliness of his behavior and relented and released.

The new jeans made me look like everyone else, and while the shame of my appearance had dissolved, a more caustic emotion (fear) was eating away at my security. Our home became an emotional battleground, causing me to become depressed. Have you ever had tears come to your eyes for no apparent reason? By the second grade, the start of each day was the same. I would sit at my desk and just cry.

One day my mother escorted my sister and me into my father's front room. The closet door was open, and only a few empty clothes hangers formed the contents of the closet. He was gone, and this is how she showed us. All that remained was the scent of his aftershave. It was a heavy moment. Her voice cracked, and tears were in her eyes as she said a word I had never heard—*divorce.* She said, "Your father and I are going to get a divorce."

The neighbors could not see behind our front door, but God could. God spells out plainly his feelings about divorce—I hate divorce. ("'I hate divorce,' says the Lord God of Israel" Malachi 2:16 NIV). If you have traveled down the road of divorce, then you know why the tender heart of the Father is pained. If you are headed down the divorce road, I pray you go the extra mile to reconcile. The emotional scars of divorce run deep, and some fifty-five years later, I believe they will last my lifetime.

My sister, my mother, and I carried on in the white frame house on Crescent Drive. Soon after the divorce, the winds of discrimination began to blow again though. Our home was owned by a retired gentleman, who had purchased the property to provide income in his retirement years. He visited with my mother one afternoon and explained that his wife did not want a divorced woman with two small children living there. We were the same people, but now we had a label that was not accepted in society at the time. Through the tears mother said, "I do not know what we are going to do."

My grandmother Pratt had given me a Bible. As a third grader with deep-seated security issues, verses in the book of Matthew drew me into prayer.

> Ask and it will be given to you; seek and you will find; knock and the door will be opened to you. For everyone who asks receives; he who seeks finds; and to him who knocks, the door will be opened. Which of you, if his son ask for bread, will give him a stone? Or if he asks for a fish, will give him a snake? If you, then, though you are evil, know how to give good gifts to your children, how much more will your Father in heaven give good gifts to those who ask him! (Matthew 7:7-11 NIV)

My third-grade theology was straightforward. I asked for security. I sought security, and I knocked on the security door. Where was God? My earthly father had left. Would my heavenly Father show up?

If you have read this far in our story, then you have asked the same question. Where is God? We are not alone in asking this question. The Psalmist did as well.

> Give ear to my words, O Lord, consider my sighing. Listen to my cry for help, My King and my God, for to you I pray. In the morning, O Lord, you hear my voice; in the morning I lay my request before you and wait in expectation. (Psalm 5:1–3 NIV)

In the morning, I would lay down my request for security before God and wait in expectation. Mama prayed too. The next morning, she went to find us an affordable place to live. She found a three-room apartment in a duplex on Fifth Avenue East. In small-town vernacular, it was on the wrong side of the tracks.

The solving of the problem of where to live led to another. How does a divorced woman with little money and no immediate family nearby move the furniture? Mama went to see the elders at the Main Street Church of Christ in Springfield, Tennessee, and presented them with the problem.

The next day God showed up wearing bib overalls and driving a pickup truck. The Main Street Church became the hands of Christ. The expectant prayer puts into play forces we cannot see and makes the invisible God become visible. There is a principle that flavors each chapter of this book, and that is that you cannot see what God is doing until you see what God has done. Need to move a mountain? Then with faith as small as a mustard seed, pray and God will show up. He may even be wearing bib overalls and driving a pickup truck.

Mama worked at boot factory, where she cut pieces from cowhides to make boots. She made ends meet unless there was a wild cat strike at the boot factory. If a strike arose, she would walk the picket line for a fraction of her take-home pay. The wild cat strike made lean times even more so.

The duplex on Fifth Avenue represented less of everything. There was less money. There were fewer friends at playtime. There was less space, as we all slept in the same room. There was less of my father. When he did visit at random and unpredictable times, he never stayed long enough to have a positive impact. His departure would be as abrupt as his arrival, always leaving a void in my heart. The one thing we had more of was the company waiting for us in the duplex. When the lights went out, the rats would explore the kitchen for food. My sister and I would set a trap and turn out the lights and wait. The trap would snap, and we would celebrate without realizing the desperation of our situation.

My Bible reading continued. The book of Matthew had yielded the principle of prayer. Jesus taught us to pray:

> Our Father in Heaven, Hallowed be your name,
> your kingdom come, your will be done on earth as it
> is in heaven. Give us today our daily bread. Forgive
> us our debts, as we also have forgiven our debtors.
> And lead us not into temptation, but deliver us
> from the evil one. (Matthew 6:9–13 NIV)

I began to pray more and more. My deeper prayer was that my Father in heaven was not a pop-in father who stopped by when it was convenient for him and not when I needed him. I prayed that God would make a way for my father to return home, to free him from the grip of the evil one. For most of my Christian life, I have prayed for God to alter circumstance. I always showed up with a list of things I wanted or things I want God to change, and this time was no different.

There were not many friends to play with on Fifth Avenue, so I spent most of my time riding my bicycle in the parking lot of Jesse Holman and Jones Hospital. The hospital was located on Brown Street, and across the street there was a large white frame house. There were two huge maple trees in the front yard that

15

laid down a cool blanket of shade below. There were three clusters of metal yard chairs where the adults would fellowship. Darting about the three clusters were dozens of children. My family had disintegrated, but this family was vibrant. There was the constant motion of the children, and every now and then a belly laugh would rise up from one of the yard chair clusters.

One summer evening before dark, I was riding my bicycle in the hospital parking lot. I stopped riding and sat watching the family across the street. Oh how I longed to be part of a family like theirs. I prayed that evening to belong to a family just like the one on Brown Street. In His time, God answered my prayer. He did not find me a family like the one I longed for. He arranged for me to join the family on Brown Street. When I prayed, I did not know that one of those ten-year-old girls playing in the front yard was Nancy Walling, and God had a plan for us.

I believe God provides three responses to our prayers. He either says yes to our request, he says to wait because the time is not right, or he says, "I have something better in mind for you." I prayed to be part of the family just like the one before my ten-year-old eyes. God had something better in mind that would far exceed my expectations.

Twelve years later on December 18, 1976, I stood at the front of Hopewell Baptist Church waiting for Nancy Walling to become my bride. My father stood beside me as my best man. A year after my hospital parking lot prayer, my father returned home, and we became a whole family again. Satan had enticed him to divide the family, but God opened doors that allowed him to return. He let God free him from the grip of the evil one.

I have pondered God deeply every day since I began my journey with him in the third grade. As I write these words some fifty-five years later, I have never found him to be a pop-in father, but constantly with me and always good.

As the doors in the back of the church opened and the organ music peaked, the most beautiful girl (inside and outside) that Robertson County ever produced came forward to be my wife. God said yes to my prayer and then some. He mended my immediate family while I waited twelve years for Nancy Walling to become Nancy Pratt. I celebrated Christmas 1976 as a member of the family on Brown Street. Notice God did not say no, but rather, "I have something better in mind for you." It took me years to piece this answered prayer together. Life was happening. I always thought I was in pursuit of God. In time I began to see clearly that He was in pursuit of me.

The days spent at the Fifth Avenue duplex were dark days filled with tears and reinforced by a constant sense of insecurity. But I know each day had purpose. I began to view elders of the church and members of the church as special people willing to help those who could not help themselves. I began to know that while I could not see God, he was in my life and calling out to me through his word, the Bible. The poverty did not go away, but the shame associated with it did fade. God was at work blocking and tackling before me. He was and is always before me.

> Your path led through the sea, your way through the mighty waters, though your foot prints were not seen. (Psalm 77:19 NIV)

17

CEDAR WAXWING

Those who look to him are radiant; their faces are never covered with shame. This poor man called, and the Lord heard him. He saved him out of all his troubles. (Psalm 34:5–6 NIV)

Moving to the duplex on Fifth Avenue was equivalent to being exiled. Life on Crescent Drive were days filled with baseball, bicycles, and horseshoe pitching. Mr. James Dean's well-manicured baseball field had been replaced by an overgrown, rat-infested vacant lot, which bordered our small backyard. The houses on Fifth Avenue were laid out with just enough street frontage to accommodate the house and a side driveway, creating a pattern that was repeated from the top of the hill, where we lived, to the bottom of the hill, where Fifth Avenue intersected Highway 41. Highway 41 was a busy four-lane US highway spanning from Florida to Wisconsin. At the duplex, the wide-open play spaces had vanished, and so had my playmates. I felt like the apostle John, exiled on the isle of Patmos.

One Saturday morning, the lack of nine-year-old fellowship drove me to make a bold move. The old neighborhood, which was rich with playmates, was about three miles away. I decided to escape. My chosen mode of transportation was my red Challenger bicycle.

In order to get to Crescent Drive, I had to travel on Highway 41 alongside semi-trucks hauling freight north and south. It was dangerous, especially for a kid on a bicycle. If I asked Mama for permission to make such a journey, I knew she would have responded with an "absolutely not" answer.

The standing Saturday morning baseball game was calling to me. The old gang was waiting for me, surely. And so, like a bird set free, I rode my bike down the hill and alongside the eighteen-wheelers until I was reunited with the old gang.

My timing this fine Saturday morning was perfect. I arrived before the all-day baseball game started. Sides were chosen by the neighborhood captains, Bubba Johnson and Terry Moulton. Bubba and Terry were captains because they were older and more experienced. They were sixth graders.

Both sides battled like juggernauts until we suspended the game for baloney sandwiches and Kool-Aid at John Weaver's house. John's house was adjacent to the baseball field and had two maples trees in the front yard, which made a shady place to enjoy our baloney and Kool-Aid.

It was a perfect day. Being with all my friends and playing baseball was about as good as it gets for a second grader. We started the afternoon session with as much energy as we had in the first ending. Our games typically went until someone's mother interrupted the game with a call to come eat supper. Late in the afternoon, it would be my mother who would interrupt our perfect Saturday baseball game.

As the afternoon progressed, there were strikeouts and base hits, along with an occasional home run. Then an odd thing occurred. A Springfield City police car turned down Crescent Drive. It was odd to see a police car because in those days, we did not lock our doors when we went somewhere. If Mama went to Kroger and forgot to turn off the pinto beans, she would put a dime in the pay phone and call Daisy Farmer, our neighbor, and ask her to turn off the beans. Daisy went through the unlocked back door to turn off the beans and save our supper.

We lived in a world without cell phones and locked doors. We lived in a world where we knew who lived in every house on Crescent Drive. We knew what the father did to make the living and each member of the household by name. We even knew the family dog or cat by name. We said, "Yes sir," and "No ma'am," when addressed by an adult. We showed respect for one another and for our neighbor's property. The police were needed at our school crossing, not in our neighborhoods.

As the police car came down alongside the baseball field, the officer began to roll down his window. We stopped the game and went toward the police car to hear what the officer had to say. As we huddled beside the car, the officer looked us over. It seemed like when he got to me, he paused for a moment. I wanted to run away and hide, because I knew that I had deliberately done wrong by darting away from the duplex without asking permission. He broke his silence with a question directed to me: "Which one of you boys is Dan Pratt?" My head dropped as my shame forced my eyes to seek the comfort of looking at the ground and not the officer.

Mama had used the long arm of the law to teach me a lesson. There were consequences associated with disobedience. About the middle of the morning, Mama missed me and noted that the bicycle was gone as well. She reasoned I had made a trip back to the old neighborhood. She called Daisy Farmer and verified I was in the Saturday morning baseball game. Mama allowed me to play all day before calling Chief Hancock to dispatch one of his police cars to bring me home.

I responded to the police officer's question with a confession, "Officer I am Dan Pratt."

He instructed, "Son, get your bicycle and I will put it in the trunk, and then get in the backseat for your ride home."

By this time the adults were outside on the porches or in the front yards to find out why a police car was in the neighborhood, and why it had stopped at the baseball field. The eyes of the neighborhood followed me into the backseat of the police cruiser. Sitting in the backseat of a police cruiser at nine years old was unforgettable. The shame of my disobedience was an unbearable weight. Tears of shame dripped onto my faded jeans. Mama, in her wisdom, provided me with an unforgettable lesson.

The police officer took me back to the Fifth Avenue duplex. Mama was waiting on the front porch. We did not have any porch furniture, so Mama was sitting on the top porch step drinking a glass of iced tea and smoking a cigarette.

Mama administered no further discipline after the officer backed out of the driveway. Mama is one of the wisest persons I have ever known. She knew that disobedience followed by the tears of shame was discipline enough. She also knew how to teach a lesson that would span a lifetime.

The rest of the summer I remained closely tethered to the Fifth Avenue duplex. The fall would bring the start of my third year in school. It was the fall of 1963. It was a dark time for me and my sister, Jane, as we were separated from friends in the old neighborhood and Mama had to be both father and mother to us.

Our home situation was dark, but circumstances would become more troubling when our president, John Kennedy, and his lovely wife, Jackie, made a trip to Dallas, Texas. Mrs. Durrett was my third-grade teacher. She came into our classroom in tears as the principal made an announcement that the president had been shot while riding in a motorcade in Dallas. A few hours later, the nation and world would mourn the passing of a beloved president and world leader. Most people on the planet can tell you where they were on November 22, 1963, and what they were doing when they heard the numbing news.

Do you remember your third-grade teacher? I remember mine well. Mrs. Durrett became more than just a teacher, and I was not just another unruly boy that filled a seat in her class. She understood that my depressed state was brought on by a broken home and depressed economic conditions for my family.

In the spring of 1964, we were assigned a project by Mrs. Durrett. We each were given a bird as the subject of a written and oral report. The bird Mrs. Durrett assigned to me was the cedar waxwing.

The cedar waxwing is a collection of silky and shiny brown, gray and lemon-yellow feathers with a black mask and brilliant-red wax droplets on the wing feathers. In the fall, they gather by the hundreds to eat berries and fill the air with their high-pitched whistles. They may have gathered by the hundreds somewhere, but not in middle Tennessee. It was rare to see a cedar waxwing on the streets of Springfield, Tennessee.

To help us learn about our bird and the birds assigned to our classmates, we were to go to Eckel's Bookstore and buy a paperback bird book that cost $1.25. When I told Mama about the book, she said we did not have $1.25 for a bird book.

Mama could have left me hanging with no book, but she did not. She called Mrs. Durrett and explained our hard times. Mrs. Durrett told Mama to have me come see her after roll call was complete the next morning. When the roll had been called, I slid from my desk and started to Mrs. Durrett's desk at the front of the room. She quietly escorted me outside the class, where no one could see a transaction that would relieve my shame of being the only child without a bird book. She gave me her bird book. The shame of my poverty was covered by a gracious heart of a third-grade teacher who loved the children she taught. I loved Mrs. Durrett because she shielded me from shame.

Tears of shame are kept in an oil can in Satan's toolbox. Whenever he wants to break us apart, he reaches for the tears of shame to lubricate our sin-corroded joints. Like Dorothy applying oil to the Tin Man in the Wizard of Oz, we spring away from our sin with a deep regret and a river of tears.

What causes tears of shame to fall to the church house floor? We are set up. God allows Satan to put us in his crosshairs and take aim at our faith. Paul writes to the Ephesians and warns them of the coming battle:

> Finally, be strong in the Lord and in his mighty power. Put on the full armor of God so that you can take your stand against the devil's schemes. For our struggle is not against flesh and blood, but against the rulers, against the authorities, against the powers of this dark world and against the spiritual forces of evil in the heavenly realms. Therefore put on the full armor of God, so that when the day of evil comes, you may be able to stand your ground, and after you have done everything, to stand. Stand firm then, with the belt of truth buckled around your waist, with the breastplate of righteousness in place, and with your feet fitted with the readiness that comes from the gospel of peace. In addition to all this, take up the shield of faith, with which you can extinguish all the flaming arrows of the evil one. (Ephesians 6:10–16 NIV)

Scripture has a story of a fellow who fell into Satan's crosshairs. He became part of the devil's schemes and the spiritual forces of darkness were cut loose. Like a chained hound that had been repeatedly beaten, Satan cut the chain to release the hound of fear, and Peter's faith was knocked off its feet.

The story begins in the upper room on a Thursday evening as Jesus, and the apostles celebrate the Passover feast. Earlier that day, Jesus had sent Peter and John ahead to make preparation for the supper. They had no money, so the conference center at the Jerusalem Marriott was not an option. With a puzzled look they asked Jesus, "Where do you want us to prepare for the supper?"

> Jesus replied, "As you enter the city, a man carrying a jar of water will meet you. Follow him to the house that he enters, and say to the owner of the house, "The Teacher asks: Where is the guest room, where I may eat the Passover with my disciples?" He will show you a large upper room, all furnished. Make preparations there." They left and found things just as Jesus had told them. So they prepared the Passover. (Luke 22:10–13 NIV)

Peter and John had seen the above principle repeated numerous times. When Jesus said events were going to unfold in a certain way, they always did.

It had been three years since Peter and John had walked away from their livelihood of fishing to follow Jesus. They left their fishing boats to become fishers of men without understanding completely what that meant (Luke 5:10–11 NIV).

Each day of those three years had been accented with miracles. They saw the dead come to life again. The widow's son, at Nain, sat up in his coffin and began to offer words of comfort to his mother (Luke 7:14–15 NIV). Their friend Lazarus, after having been dead for four days, came forth from the tomb still bound by his grave clothes (John 11:38–43 NIV). Peter, James, and John witnessed the ashen face of Jairus's daughter turn rosy as she arose from her death bed (Mark 5:36–42 NIV). In all three cases, Jesus spoke and the dead came to life. Peter, James, and John as fishermen had struggled against the waves and wind to get to a safe harbor. They had witnessed Jesus use not the oar but the spoken word to calm the sea and bring them to safety (Mark 4:35–41 NIV). They had seen it all. All things were possible for Jesus.

This week had started with a victory parade into Jerusalem. Jesus sat on a colt and the people spread their cloaks and branches on the road before him. They shouted,

> Hosanna! Blessed is he who comes in the name of the Lord! Blessed is the coming kingdom of our father David! Hosanna in the highest! (Mark 11:9–10 NIV)

Peter and the other disciples believed that their dedication in following Jesus was about to pay a handsome dividend. It did, but in a way they could not understand at that time. Years later, the old apostle would write of the payout as a gift that filled him with inexpressible and glorious joy (1 Peter 1:8 NIV).

As the Passover supper continued, Peter's brow wrinkled as he tried to associate the victorious entry into Jerusalem on Sunday with Jesus's words around the supper table.

> When the hour came, Jesus and his apostles reclined at the table. And he said to them, "I have eagerly desired to eat this Passover with you before I suffer. For I tell you, I will not eat it again until it finds fulfillment in the kingdom of God." (Luke 22:14–16 NIV)

There were a number of times when the apostles did not understand what Jesus was saying. This was one of those times. Peter did not relate the victorious entry with suffering. Jesus went on to talk about a memorial service to remember him using bread and wine as symbols. Why was Jesus talking about suffering when he should have been talking about a Roman downfall and the new order of governance in Jerusalem? Peter and the others certainly wanted to have that conversation, because an argument broke out among them as to who was the greatest (Luke 22:24 NIV). They wanted to talk cabinet positions, not what was sounding like a disastrous ending of their three-year investment.

As Peter pondered Jesus's words, the Lord hit him with a bucket of emotional cold water. Peter, rather than being named as secretary of state, you are about to be painfully tested.

> "Simon, Simon, Satan has asked to sift you as wheat. But I have prayed for you, Simon, that your faith may not fail. And when you have turned back, strengthen your brothers." But he replied, "Lord, I am ready to go with you to prison and to death." Jesus answered, "I tell you, Peter, before the rooster crows today, you will deny three times that you know me." (Luke 22:31–34 NIV)

Satan would sift Peter as he would have crushed wheat. All the good parts of Peter would fall through Satan's sieve, leaving only the chaff, which represented all that was bad in Peter. In Rudyard Kipling's poem "If," the poet writes:

> If you can bare to hear the truth you have spoken
> Twisted by knaves to make a trap for fools.

Peter was to have an encounter with the chief knave, which would take his bold promise to not abandon Jesus even if it cost him prison or death and make a fool out of Peter. Peter was on a journey that would end in tears of shame. He would not be able to bear the truth that he denied knowing Jesus not one but three times. In one of the most chilling scenes in the Bible, the reality of Peter's denial is sealed by a look of love across a courtyard when the third wave of denial crested.

> Then seizing him, they led him away and took him to the house of the high priest. Peter followed

27

at a distance. But when they had kindled a fire in the middle of the courtyard and had sat down together, Peter sat down with them. A servant girl saw him there seated in the fire light. She looked closely at him and said' "This man was with him." But he denied it. "Woman, I don't know him," he said. A little time later someone else saw him and said, "You also are one of them." "Man I am not!" Peter replied. About an hour later another asserted, "Certainly this fellow was with him for he is a Galilean." Peter replied, "Man, I don't know what you are talking about!" Just as he was speaking, the rooster crowed. The Lord turned and looked straight at Peter. Then Peter remembered the word that the Lord had spoken to him: "Before the rooster crows today, you will disown me three times." And he went outside and weep bitterly. (Luke 22:54–62 NIV)

Jesus did not cast a condemning look at Peter. Jesus knew the chief knave well and the level to which he would go to crush a man. Peter had taken such a bold stand that the denials caused not just weeping, but bitter weeping. Peter went into hiding and wept until there just were not any more tears. When you get to that point, then there is a trembling that takes control of the body. In the next chapter I will write of a time when I had no more tears, only trembling. Just as Jesus cast a look of love toward Peter, my God would show up for me in a time of trembling.

A broken Peter was being positioned to be a church leader. Jesus had prayed that his faith would not fail. Jesus is at the right hand of the Father praying that same prayer for you and me today (Romans 8:34 NIV). An untested faith is a weaker faith. The testing of faith can be painful, as Peter's experience demonstrates. Perhaps you were like me at nine years old. You knew right from wrong, but you chose wrong. The result was tears of shame. Is your faith being tested as Peter's was? Jesus is praying for you. Reach out and take hold of his nail-pierced hand and be forgiven. He came that we might have life and have it to the full (John 10:10 NIV), not for us to have a life of shame and regret.

Many years have passed since Mama turned me into the law. I was a strongheaded young man in need of a humbling lesson. Having the eyes of the neighborhood on me as I entered the police cruiser made me feel ashamed, and it was a feeling I never wanted to experience again. As an engineer, my work has allowed me to travel the world. I have been on five continents, and I never leave for a distant land without calling Mama to let her know where I will be. It was a lesson that stuck.

PS: Folks often ask me if I was ever in the US military. I reply, "I never was in our great military, but I was raised by a marine drill sergeant named Margaret."

Thanks, Mama!

BILL THOMAS

As the dear pants for streams of water, so my soul pants for you, O God. My soul thirst for God, the living God. When can I go and meet with God? My tears have been my food day and night, while men say to me all day long, "Where is your God?" (Psalm 42:1–3 NIV)

Have you ever had a day that made you want to whistle? If whistling is not how you express deep-felt joy, perhaps you sing or hum a familiar tune. If life were a roller coaster ride, you would be in the first car on the highest summit of the ride, with a big grin on your face. Life at the summit is sweet because you have absolutely no regrets. All your projects would be ahead of schedule and below budget, with a perfect safety record. Attending the family reunion would be an event that would keep you awake at night as you anticipated positive interactions from a family that was in perfect harmony. There would be no need to win the lottery because you have enough resources to last for the rest of your life. The need to climb one more rung on the social ladder to improve your standing would not be possible because there were no more rungs left to climb. You would feel good all the time. Your health would be so good that you have never had bad breath. What if you linked all your days together and each one was like this extraordinary day?

A life like this would not be possible. Even a fraction of this life is out of reach for most of us. You may further protest by pointing out that the fellow described above is so outlandish, he would have an address in the Emerald City in the Land of Oz. There is a fellow like this described in the Bible, though. He did not live in the Land of Oz but in the Land of Uz.

> In the land of Uz there lived a man whose name was Job. This man was blameless and upright; he feared God and shunned evil. He had seven sons and three daughters, and he owned seven thousand sheep, three thousand camels, five hundred yoke of oxen and five hundred donkeys, and had a large number of servants. He was the greatest man among all the people of the East. His sons used to hold feasts in their homes on their birthdays, and they would invite their three sisters to eat and drink with them. When a period of feasting had run its course, Job would send and have them purified. Early in the morning he would sacrifice a burnt offering for each of them, thinking, "Perhaps my children have sinned and cursed God in their hearts." This was Job's regular custom. (Job 1:1–5 NIV)

Job had it all! We could not add anything to the list that would have made his life richer and his state of mind more peaceful. He was a righteous man who feared God and shunned evil.

Let me tell you a story about a time such as this in my family. Life was not just good; life was great. Nancy and I had been married for thirty-eight years. She was my eighth-grade sweetheart. When people who know I am from Tennessee hear that they often ask, did we get married in the eighth grade?

We had two sons who were now grown and well established.

The oldest son, Bill, is a hard worker in the grocery business. He was a bagger at the HEB in Boerne, Texas, and well known in our community. He has a delightful personality. Nancy and I were proud of all Bill's accomplishments. Our youngest son, Joshua, was in his fourth year of a five-year residency to become a general surgeon. He had married his college sweetheart, Celeste. They had both finished a successful undergraduate program at Harding University and were married while Joshua was in medical school. After medical school, they moved to Chicago, where Joshua learned the craft of being a surgeon and Celeste was an architectural designer for a major firm located in downtown Chicago. Life on the home front could not have been better.

My work was going well. I was working for a major heavy industrial engineering and construction firm. My current project was the largest and most interesting in a career that had spanned thirty-five years. Retirement was approaching, and the Lord had blessed me with continuous employment, so the funds for retirement were adequate. Life on the work front could not have been better.

Perhaps the most satisfying part of my life was my affiliation with Oak Hills Church. I had been an elder in that church for the past ten years and had the deep privilege of teaching the Mountain Climbers class for the past twelve. The Mountain Climbers class is made of the seniors at Oak Hills. They have an unshakable faith. They have taken all the trials this life can throw at you and remained faithful to the God they love. My fellow elders, Doyle Jennings and Rick Nicosia, and I had been blessed with an opportunity to go to Fredericksburg, Texas, to start a branch of the Oak Hills Church in that community. God richly blessed the work in Fredericksburg. God continued to draw men unto himself through the Oak Hills Church such that a major building program was needed to keep pace with a steady stream of believers. Life on the church front could not have been better.

One evening, while Nancy and I were on our deck overlooking Boerne Lake, we received a phone call from Joshua. Nancy answered, and I could tell from the smile on her face and the rebel yell she made that the news was good. Joshua and Celeste were going to have a child. Good times just got better! In the movie *Gone with the Wind*, Miss Melanie learned that Scarlet had had a daughter, and they named her Bonnie Blue Butler. Miss Melanie, whose voice was seasoned with joy, exclaimed, "Oh the best days are the days when babies come!" Our best days were on the horizon.

After that call, our family went into baby mode. The first child of the next generation was en route to a family aching for a little one to raise and adore. Ultrasound pictures adorned our refrigerator. Joshua and Celeste bought a baby crib. Nancy started to work on a patchwork blanket. I pondered opening an account for my first grandchild's college education.

Each doctor visit yielded a fresh ultrasound picture for the refrigerator. Each visit brought the good news that all was well, which traveled across the family in a burst of text messages. The folks at Northwest Church of Christ, where Joshua and Celeste attended, organized a baby shower. The whole church wanted to express their love through the giving of gifts. Nancy bought her airline ticket weeks in advance of the shower that was set for the middle of March. At thirty-two weeks into the pregnancy, all dashboard lights were flashing green, and our family awaited the birth of our first grandson.

My work routine had me leaving home on Monday and returning on Friday evening. This well-established routine was interrupted on March 16, 2015. I had spent the day working from the San Antonio office. I was whistling and having a Mr. Bluebird on my shoulder kind of moment as I left work to go home for supper. Nancy was shopping at HEB, getting items for a special "Dan is home on Monday night" dinner. As I turned down the driveway, my cell phone began to vibrate. I have a hard rule of no cell phone if the vehicle is in motion. By the time I reached the end of the driveway and stopped the vehicle, the phone had stopped vibrating. The call had been from Joshua.

Bill answered our house phone as I entered the front door. He had a wild look in his eye and handed me the phone and said, "It is Josh." Bill's look tipped me off that all was not right.

I said, "Hello."

My hello was met with a one-syllable word: "Dad." Joshua spoke only one word and released a tidal wave of emotion.

"Yes, son, what is the matter?" I quickly responded.

"Dad, we lost the baby," Joshua sobbed.

The news was not a mile marker on the roadway of life. It was an emotional moment frozen at absolute zero on the span of life. There was not a molecule of hope in motion. The child was dead. We wept.

We regained our composure, and Joshua outlined the critical facts. "We are at the hospital. The baby stopped moving yesterday, which was unusual, so we came into to see the doctor. The medical team has determined the child has no heartbeat and will be stillborn."

As I hung up the phone, my mind raced as to how to tell Nancy and what should we do to support Joshua and Celeste. It is rare that Nancy and I come into the same room without big smiles flashing between us. When Nancy came through the garage door, she flashed a big smile that faded when she saw my downcast appearance. Without a word being spoken by me, she said, "What is wrong?"

"Joshua called to tell us that they lost the baby," I said. I gave Nancy the few details that I had, and then we wept.

We put the tears aside for a short while and began to make plans. The ticket purchased for the baby shower would be used to go to Chicago and support Joshua and Celeste. We bought a ticket thinking a great celebration was in the works, not knowing instead the services of a funeral director would be required. I would stay at home with Bill and support him. Bill does not break out of his work routine well, nor does he like to travel.

On March 17, 2015, our first grandchild was born. He was a motionless little boy delivered into a grieving family. He was named Bill Thomas after his uncle Bill. Nancy and I had named our first son Bill in honor of my father. Joshua chose to honor his brother by naming his first son Bill.

Nancy did all the heavy lifting in Chicago as she tried to comfort Joshua and Celeste. Their expectations had been crushed. Baby things had to be put out of sight, and arrangements for the cremation of Bill Thomas had to be made. Our family took comfort from God's assurance that he was close by in our time of pain.

> The Lord is close to the brokenhearted and saves
> those that are crushed in spirit. (Psalm 34:18 NIV)

The next day God would demonstrate to me in a personal way that he was near.

Nancy and I talked several times each day. I was hungry for news about Joshua and Celeste, and Nancy needed some encouragement as she led our family through a grief-stricken valley. After one such call, I went out on the deck overlooking the lake. Bill was at work, so I was alone. The grief began to roll into my soul like angry waves pushed by a hurricane. Wave after wave pounded my emotions, producing a flow of tears that dotted the deck beneath my rocking chair. After a while, there were no more tears left, and I began to just tremble.

It was March 18, the first day away from Nancy and the day after Bill Thomas's birth. As I sat trembling and heaped up in my rocking chair, I heard the singing of birds. The tree alongside the dog run behind the house was just starting to leaf out. The leaves were so few that I could see the lake through the tree branches. As I wept, the tree had been filling with songbirds because there were no birds in the tree when I went out on the deck. The tree had well over a hundred birds singing with a familiar high-pitched whistling sound. I adjusted my glasses, and the bird sitting in the top of the tree came into focus. It was a cedar waxwing! My eyes moved from one bird to another, confirming that they all were cedar waxwings. Our black lab, Lou, also took notice of the birds. Nancy spent a week in Chicago, and each day the birds came to sing to me and Lou.

Seeing cedar waxwings on Boerne Lake was beyond rare. In twelve years of fishing on the lake and gardening beside the lake, I had never seen a cedar waxwing. I reasoned to myself, "Why had the cedar waxwing not crossed my mind since Mrs. Durrett's third-grade class?" The dots began to connect! When I was first introduced to the Cedar Waxwing, it was a dark night of the soul time in my life. It was life in the duplex on Fifth Avenue. Another dark night of the soul had just overshadowed me, and God, through the cedar waxwing, was sending me a message.

In the Bible there is a story of a judge named Gideon who asked God for a sign to reassure him of God's presence. God granted Gideon a sign of his presence. In a respectful manner Gideon asked God for a second sign of his presence. A second sign was granted (Judges 6:33–40 NIV).

I did not ask God for a sign of his presence. But our family was passing through the valley of the shadow of death.

> Even though I walk through the valley of the
> shadow of death, I will fear no evil, for you are
> with me; your rod and your staff, they comfort
> me. (Psalm 23:4 NIV)

In my dark night of the soul moment, God sent me a sign that only I could understand. The sign had been fifty years in the making. The sign came at the right time. His message was clear! *I was with you in the darkest hour of your young life, and now*

that you are age sixty, I am still here. I did not request the sign of
the cedar waxwing, but it was sent by a God who is close to the
brokenhearted and those crushed in spirit.

This part of the story is not about asking or not asking God
for a sign of his presence. It is intended to show the character of
God. God does not change like shifting shadows. He is constantly
good in a world that is unfair and touched by the infected fingers
of Satan (James 1:17 NIV).

God is not distant. He always keeps his promises. There is a
precious promise found in the Hebrew letter.

> Never will I leave you. Never will I forsake you.
> (Hebrews 13:5 NIV)

We typically plan our lives in such a way as to avoid painful
detours. We are given the deep privilege of choice by our God. We
can choose to apply ourselves in the area of education and reap the
financial benefits of a solid education. We chose our mate with an
eye toward a harmonious life together and the raising of the next
generation. We make health choices that lead to a richer, fuller
life. How do we respond when all the right choices still lead to
an unexpected detour? In a later chapter of this book, we will see
that Job made all the right choices, but his life spun out of control
despite his righteousness.

God's provision goes beyond our planning. The cedar waxwing
lay dormant in my life until God was ready to use it fifty years
later. Jesus told a story of a wise man who planned well and built
his house on a rock. The storms came and assaulted the house,
and it stood firm. A foolish man planned poorly and built his
house on the sand. The storms came too, and destroyed the house.
The point of the story is that we may trust in the wisdom of God
and not our own, because there will be storms. The storms are
not optional, for Jesus said, "In this world you will have trouble.
But take heart! I have overcome the world" (John 16:33 NIV).

The nature of God is always good, even when our circumstances take an unexpected detour. One of the best insights I have into the nature of God came from a story time with the fifth graders at Oak Hills. Miss Ann was the song leader, and I was asked to tell a Bible story. When we had finished our songs, Miss Ann asked for prayer request. One bright little fellow shot his hand into the air and began to squirm in anticipation of gaining Miss Ann's attention. When called upon, he blurted out, "Miss Ann, my dog died, and I want to know if there will be dogs in heaven." The lad could have posed his question to the best theological minds on the planet and would not have gotten a more profound answer. Miss Ann responded, "The Bible does not say one way or the other as to the presence of dogs in heaven. My dog died too. I loved him, and like you, I was sad to see him pass. Since the Bible is silent, I really do not know if my precious dog will be in heaven when I arrive. But I do know my God." She went on, "My God is good, and he loves to surprise me with good things. When I get to heaven, I believe that my dog will be sitting beside Jesus waiting for me." The little fellow was satisfied with Miss Ann's explanation. I was impressed. I am not sure about allowing cats in heaven, but I too believe that my ole Lou dog will be sitting beside Jesus waiting for me. We have a good, good Father!

There will be more than a beloved dog to greet me when I step into heaven. There will be my first grandson, Bill Thomas, there as well. I never got to know him in this life, but I will have eternity to spend with him in the next life. Our God is so very good!

MAMA JEANNIE

Taste and see that the LORD is good; blessed is the man that takes refuge in him. Fear the LORD, you his saints, for those who fear him lack nothing. The lions may grow weak and hungry, but those who seek the LORD lack no good thing. Come my children, listen to me; I will teach you the fear of the LORD. (Psalm 34:8–11 NIV)

Hopewell Baptist Church, located in northern Robertson County, Tennessee, is a holy place for our family. Nancy grew up in that church and played the piano during worship as a teenager. Later, Nancy and I were married at Hopewell on a snowy night in December 1976. In 2013, we laid our father, Louis Walling, to rest in the Hopewell Cemetery, and on this day we had come to lay our mother, Nancy Jean Walling, to rest. Nancy and I plan on joining them there when it is our time to meet Jesus face-to-face. It was at Hopewell, standing before Brother Elmer Mason, that Nancy and I promised to have and to hold one another till death do us part, and someday there will be a stone marker in Hopewell Cemetery with our names inscribed upon it to validate that truth. Fifteen years after Brother Mason married us, we saw him at a reunion. By that time Nancy and I had two boys racing around the church building. As Brother Mason watched our boys, he leaned in toward me and said, "Looks like I tied that knot pretty good."

Hopewell was not just a holy place for our family but has also served in that capacity for hundreds and hundreds of other families over its more than 150 years of ministering to the community. It has always been, and probably will always be, a small country church where everyone knows one another. For generations, when folks thought about Hopewell, they thought about going home.

While Nancy was growing up at Hopewell, I spent time visiting my grandmother Pratt's small rural church. Grandmother Pratt and Uncle Joe and his family attended Mount Sharon Upper Cumberland Presbyterian Church. Both of these small churches were the center of community life. The church was where we fellowshipped, worshiped, married, and said our last goodbyes to friends and family.

Like most country churches, Hopewell and Mount Sharon always held a homecoming each summer with a potluck dinner following worship. I hope that the feast in heaven that Jesus promised us is as good. There was a fellow who only came to church one time a year at Mount Sharon; he came for homecoming. His dress was a bit shabby, and he smelled of sour sweat. He had great timing, in his eyes, as he would arrive and sit on the back row just as the preacher was finishing his sermon. He was always just in time for dinner.

Small country churches have a unique character. I remember the heat of summer that made sitting still and listening to a fire-and-brimstone sermon difficult for most everyone, especially a boy like me. There was no air conditioning, so the large stained-glass windows would be raised in the summertime. On occasion, a breeze would send some relief to the hot, sticky congregation. With the windows raised, invariably a bee or a wasp would fly into the church, which always made for some good southern entertainment. The wasp would hover over the congregation, buzzing overhead, while the preacher would have to compete for their attention and pretend to ignore the wasp as well. The wasp became the center of attention despite the pulpit-pounding efforts of the preacher.

On the back of each pew was a holder for the songbooks and Bibles, along with a fan to help with that summer heat. The fan handle was made of an expanded popsicle stick with a stiff piece of smooth cardboard either glued or stapled to the stick. On one side was a picture of Da Vinci's *Last Supper* and on the other an advertisement for the local funeral home. The preachers of the day had to be extra talented to maintain their concentration while addressing a congregation fluttering fans as they watched a wasp hover overhead. Every now and then, the wasp would descend upon one of the beehive hairdos of one of the church sisters. A helpful neighbor would swat at the wasp, causing the sister to holler out loud and bring the preacher to a pause as the congregation came to order.

Thoughts of the sights and sounds from the many years at Hopewell floated across my mind as I stood by Mama Jeannie's grave that January day. The folks were parking their cars and adjusting their clothes as they made their way to the graveside. Along with her grandsons sharing tributes and leading songs of remembrance, I had been given the deep privilege of preaching Mama Jeannie's funeral. I'd like to share what I had to say with you, reader, as well.

Nancy Jean Freeman Walling

December 5, 1931–January 2, 2016

We gather here at Hopewell Baptist Church this morning not to focus on the date of birth or death but on the dash that separates those two dates. The dash between those two dates represents a life. In the case of Nancy Jean, it was a life well lived.

Journey with me back to Brown Street. There was a white-framed house that was across the street from Jessie Holman Jones Hospital. It was where Big Momma and Papa lived. It was the place Nancy Jean and her five sisters and three brothers called home.

Let's take a position on Brown Street and see Nancy Jean and her sister Martha Bea roller-skating down the sidewalk or watch Nancy Jean twirl her baton in the front yard. Listen closely and you can hear Nancy Jean dribbling a basketball. Lift up our eyes to observe Louis Walling picking up Nancy Jean for a trip to Russellville, Kentucky, where, in the company of Buck and Martha Bea, they would be married. If a poet stood with us he would apply the term carpe diem to the life of Nancy Jean, for she seized each day and lived it to the full.

My first visit to Brown Street was in 1963. At that time my mother, sister, and I were living in a three-room duplex on Fifth Avenue. Our family life was in distress. I would ride my bicycle in the hospital parking lot and observe this wonderful, harmonious family across Brown Street. The front yard was dotted with white yard chairs sitting in the shade of maple trees, and there were kids running in all directions. The laughter was contagious and could be heard across the street. I remember praying to God to be a part of a family that loved being together and laughing. Little did I realize that God would help me connect the dots with one of these little girls. Her name too is Nancy.

Mama Jeannie is the last member of that great family to step into the presence of Jesus. Somewhere in paradise is a white-framed house with maple trees and yard chairs, and Tooter, Martha Bea, Big Momma, Annie Laurie, and the whole gang are laughing and cutting up.

Momma Jeannie would leave Brown Street at the age of seventeen to marry Louis Walling, and like Big Momma, she would become the mother of a large family. There would be countless trips to Dr. Stone's office with a sick child and countless hours spent nursing Louis through surgeries and sickness. As a homemaker, she would make the trip to City Cash Grocery in a taxi cab and face mountains of dirty dishes and diapers. She did it all with love.

How best to capture Momma Jeannie's dash? Her story was centered in family, and her life was centered in Christ.

Each Christmas before gifts were opened, Momma Jeannie would ask one of us to turn to the book of Luke and read the birth story of Christ. She wanted all the young ones to hear the story. She believed in the promises of God and wanted her children and grandchildren to grasp the power in those promises just as she had done. Listen to those promises.

- Never will I leave you, never will I forsake you. (Hebrews 13:5 NIV)
- Even though I walk through the valley of the shadow of death I will fear no evil for you are with me. (Psalm 23:4 NIV)
- Precious in the sight of the Lord is the death of his saints. (Psalm 116:15 NIV)
- I lift up my eyes unto the hills, where does my help come from? My help comes from the Lord maker of heaven and earth. (Psalm 121:1 NIV)

She wanted us to know God because she found him to be an ever-present help in time of trouble (Psalm 46:1). Lean forward and listen to a message from the Bible to which Momma Jeannie would say Amen!

Psalm 34:11 (NIV): "Come, my children, listen to me; I will teach you the fear of the Lord."

Psalm 34:6–10 (NIV): "This poor man called, and the Lord heard him; he saved him out of his troubles. The angel of the

LORD encamps around those who fear him, and he delivers them. Taste and see that the LORD is good; blessed is the man who takes refuge in him. Fear the LORD, you his saints, for those who fear him lack nothing. The lions may grow weak and hungry, but those who seek the Lord lack no good thing."

Psalm 34:11 (NIV): "Come, my children, listen to me; I will teach you the fear of the Lord."

Psalm 34:12–22 (NIV): "Whoever of you loves life and desires to see many good days, keep your tongue from evil and your lips from speaking lies, turn from evil and do good; seek peace and pursue it. The eyes of the LORD are on the righteous and his ears are attentive to their cry; the face of the LORD is against those who do evil, to cut off the memory of them from the earth. The righteous cry out, and the LORD hears them; he delivers them from their troubles. The LORD is close to the brokenhearted and saves those who are crushed in spirit. A righteous man may have many troubles, but the LORD delivers him from them all; he protects all his bones, not one of them will be broken. Evil will slay the wicked; the foes of the righteous will be condemned. The LORD redeems his servants; no one will be condemned who takes refuge in him."

When my remarks were finished, the funeral director took charge and concluded the service. The pall was removed from the casket, which was an arrangement of flowers made especially for Mama Jeannie. In memory of her favorite bird, the arrangement included dozens of white roses interspersed with tiny figurines of red cardinals. The crowd began to visit and meander back to their cars for the trip back to town, and I left Hopewell Cemetery knowing that someday it would be my turn to have words spoken over me. What would they say about the way I spent my life, my dash?

The next day we made our way back to Nashville for the two-hour flight back to San Antonio. The flight went well, but the weather in San Antonio was dreary. The gray sky touched the ground, and mist collected on the windshield as we drove back home to Boerne. The ride home was quiet. We had spent the last few weeks with Mama Jeannie in the hospital, and then passing, so we left each other alone with our own thoughts. Pulling into the driveway lifted our spirits as we were at last at home.

We unloaded the car in the rain. As we came through the front door, we encountered a spectacular sight. Our house faces north, overlooking Boerne Lake, and the north side is framed with large windows. There is a wow effect as you step through the front door into the presence of the lake. On this day, the effect went from *wow* to *amazing*. The tree alongside the dog run was full of birds. There were over a hundred cedar waxwing birds in the same tree that they occupied the week after Bill Thomas's birth and passing. This time it was slightly different from the Bill Thomas event: in the center of the tree was the biggest red cardinal bird in the state of Texas.

I may exaggerate my comparisons at times, but Nancy made pictures of this amazing sight or else it might be hard to believe. For the next several minutes, we sat at the kitchen table and marveled at the birds and the goodness of the Father who had sent them. Another time of grief had overshadowed our family. On January 3, 2016, God sent cedar waxwings to assure us that he was standing shoulder to shoulder with us in our Valley of the Shadow of Death experience, just as he was when Bill Thomas passed.

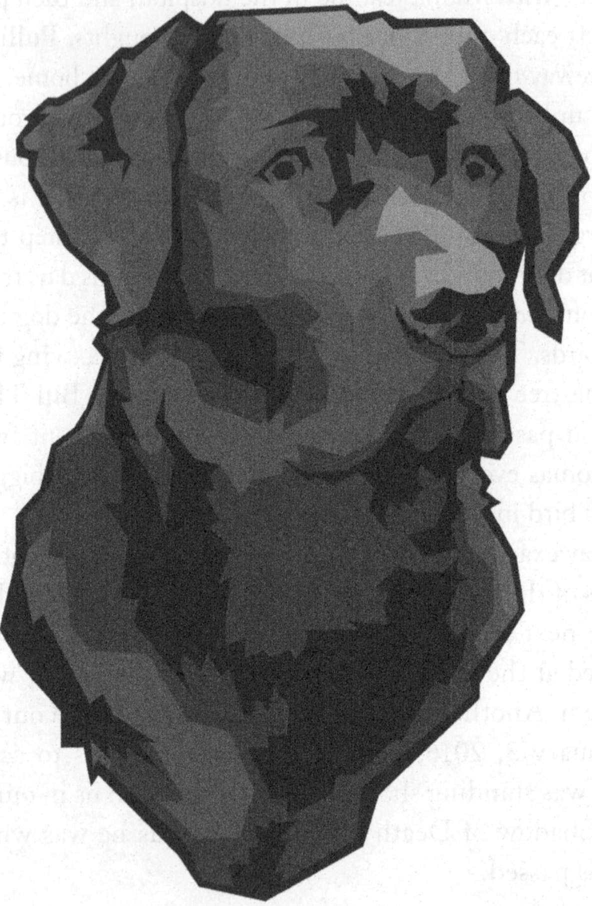

OLE BLACK DOGS

A man of many companions may come to ruin, but
there is a friend that sticks closer than a brother.
(Proverbs 18:24 NIV)

Have you ever had to say a final goodbye to a pet? On more
than one occasion, I have prayed with folks who have tried
to readjust their life after a pet passes. The church house floor
has been stained with tears as folks recall those big brown eyes
set into a tilted head. They often share, "The dog was always so
glad to see me. Time did not make any difference. If I took the
garbage out, or had been away all day, when I came through the
door, I was met with a bark of joy and a wagging tail." For my
family, we have a soft spot for black dogs, and any time I see one,
it lifts my spirits.

We said goodbye to two different black dogs over the years.
The first black dog was inherited from a British family when we
were in Spain on a work assignment. His name was Jack, and he
was a junkyard dog. In his early days, he roamed from Dumpster
to Dumpster to survive. Years later, the second black dog was
purchased to mend the heart of our youngest son, Joshua, when
we had to say goodbye to ole Jack. His name was Lou, and he was
a pedigree black Labrador. His mother was a chocolate Labrador
who delivered a litter of all-black pups. When Lou tilted that

blocky little head at me for the first time, all the other puppies in the litter faded away.

When we first arrived in Spain, Joshua was ten years old. My routine at that time was to spend the work week in Madrid and return to Sotogrande in southern Spain on the weekends. The first time that I came home from Madrid, there was a large black dog lying on the back doormat. I said, "That ol' black dog looks like he is right at home lying on our back doormat." Joshua beamed as he explained how Jack came our way: the British family had rescued Jack from his Dumpster days along the Sotogrande harbor, but they were returning to England. Upon arriving in England, a foreign dog had to be quarantined for six months before being released to his family. They could not stand the thought of a free-ranging Spanish dog being in a cage for that long, so they talked the new Americans in to taking him.

Joshua was having a difficult time adjusting to all the newness in his life in Spain, but Jack's arrival changed Joshua's outlook on life. He had a new best friend who made the sun shine again for Joshua. There are fewer bonds stronger than the bond between a ten-year-old boy and his dog. I believe Joshua's transformation was divinely arranged by the sending of an ol' black dog as his constant companion.

Joshua and his older brother, Bill, went to the international school in Sotogrande. Before becoming a school, it had been a working Spanish farm with a large workers' quarters. Repurposed to be classrooms, the quarters were built in a square, with an open courtyard in the center. The courtyard had a fountain in the center where the sound of falling water made a great setting in which to learn.

Joshua and Bill would jump on their bicycles in the morning for the trip to school, and ol' Jack would come to attention from his back doormat post and follow them. The classrooms around the courtyard did not intimidate Jack. When Joshua went in for class, Jack would follow close behind and take up a post outside of the classroom until Joshua returned. In the States, this boy/ dog relationship would have not been allowed inside the school. A platoon of mamas would have surely mounted their SUVs for an attack on this special boy/dog treatment. Fortunately for Jack, we were not in America; we were in an international school where diversity was not something that we strived to achieve. It was simply a way of life.

Miss Sue was Joshua's teacher in Sotogrande. She had watched Joshua struggle to function normally in school since arriving, and each of those early days in school brought tears for him. Joshua had not moved to a new school but rather a new school in a different country. There were fourteen children in Joshua's class representing seven nationalities. One day everyone is speaking Tennessean, and then after a long airplane ride, they are speaking Dutch, German, Russian, Greek, French, Spanish, and English. Joshua's new normal was not just different; it was frankly unsettling for a ten-year-old. Miss Sue had keen instincts and realized that the bond between Joshua and Jack was the emotional medicine needed to get our son back in the game.

Joshua had his Miss Sue, and I had my Mrs. Durrett. Both were special teachers who reached out to teach more than simply history and math. Special teachers are those who understand the emotions that make a ten-year-old tick in a supercharged peer pressure environment.

When we adopted Jack into our home, Nancy was also given an opportunity to be a special teacher at the international school. Miss Linda was the mother of the British family that had rescued Jack from his junkyard dog days, and when she brought Jack to our house, she also brought two cardboard boxes full of Bible teaching materials. At the international school, each week the Catholic children went with the priest to prepare for their first communion service. Miss Linda had taken the remaining forty-plus children to share Bible stories. Miss Linda asked Nancy to take her dog and her Bible class, and Nancy agreed. Our family had a new best friend in ol' Jack, and the hearts of children grew closer to God though the teaching of the Bible.

We went to Spain thinking that the building of two chemical plants was the main reason for the adventure, but we left Spain knowing that the engineering work was a cheap sideshow. Under the big top tent, Nancy was teaching young minds the basic blocking and tackling stories from God's word. God tells us through the prophet Isaiah that his word always has an impact:

> As the rain and the snow come down from heaven,
> and do not return to it without watering the earth
> and making it bud and flourish, so that it yields
> seed for the sower and bread for the eater, so is
> my word that goes out from my mouth: It will not
> return to me empty, but will accomplish what I
> desire and achieve the purpose for which I sent it.
> (Isaiah 55:10–11 NIV)

We will never know on this side of heaven the impact that God's word had on those children, and neither do we know the impact on the generations that would rise up from those children. The headliner show was under the big top, where it did not entertain the audience but changed them forever.

As our time in Spain drew to a close, I stayed behind with ol' Jack and the family returned to our home in Kingsport, Tennessee. I had the last chemical plant to finish and commission, and Nancy reopened our home. She had to remove all the sheets that had covered the furniture for the past five years and do some old-fashioned spring cleaning. The windows went up, and the Pine Sol came out. She also had an invisible fence installed around the perimeter of the yard so Jack would have plenty of room when the last leg of the Pratt family returned home.

Ol' Jack spent years under the deep blue skies of southern Spain, where in the five years we lived there, we never saw a frost.

But he adapted to the Tennessee weather well. He grew gray around the mouth and on the tops of his paws.

In Jack's second Tennessee summer, Joshua left on a Sunday for a mission trip to Mexico. On Monday about noon, ol' Jack laid down for the last time under the picnic table on the patio. When Joshua returned home the next week, I went to pick him up at the church, which was about ten minutes from our house. As we left the church parking lot, I gave Joshua the news. There were no words at first, only tears, as they rolled across his cheeks and dripped from his chin onto his lap. The bond between a boy and his dog forms quickly and lasts a lifetime. In time, the tears stopped, but the bond they had is eternal.

At work the next day, I shared our loss with one of the mechanics. Jerry's eyes teared up, and he said, "I have lost several dogs. It always hurts. The best medicine is another dog. I have a friend that has a litter of black Labrador puppies in a horse barn on the Holston River."

A week after Jack's passing, Joshua and I went to the horse barn on the Holston to see this black mass of puppies. The alpha male stood out, as Joshua picked him up and said, "Dad, this is my new dog, and we are going to call him Lou after granddaddy Louis Walling." That day was the beginning of a sixteen-year journey with another black dog.

There is a tractor-trailer load of stories about Lou that span our sixteen years together. Let's summarize them by saying there is something about an ol' black dog that warms the heart year in and year out and breaks it the day he passes.

Nancy called work to tell me Lou was in his doghouse and did not have the strength to get out. Like ol' Jack, Lou had grown gray around the mouth and on the tops of his paws. I left work thinking this might be the day that we said goodbye to Lou.

When I arrived at home, my neighbor, Todd Nye, helped me with Lou. First we had to disassemble the doghouse by removing the top so we could help Lou try and stand. He was old, immobile, and miserable, so Todd and I put him in the dog carrier and moved him to a pickup truck for the ride to the vet's office in Boerne, Texas.

When we arrived at the vet's office, I carried Lou through the back door and into an examination room, where we made a pallet out of large bath towels for Lou on the floor. The vet said some comforting things to us about a lab that was hearty enough to make the sixteen-year mark. It was time to say goodbye, so Nancy and I left the office through the same back door, both of us in tears. Nancy sobbed and asked, "This is the first time I have left this office without them swiping my credit card. Do we need to go back inside?" (We did not—they knew where to find us.)

Bill and I did some shopping when I came to get him from work that day. I decided that I would wait until we were out of the HEB grocery store before I told him that Lou was down. As my mind drifted and I reasoned that tears shed outside his workplace would be best, I heard Bill's cell phone ring. I could tell from the conversation it was Nancy calling from home. My mind kicked in, and I began to think that she had another item for the shopping list. Instead, Bill handed me the phone, saying, "She wants to tell you something."

Nancy's message was not about a grocery list. She said, "They are back!" I made a reply about not understanding, so Nancy responded, "The cedar waxwings are in the same tree down by the dog run, and Dan, there are a hundred of them, just like when Bill Thomas and Mama Jeannie passed."

Grief had paid our house a visit three times over the past year, and God sent a sign of connection each of the three times. It was a sign that was personal for me because the cedar waxwing story began fifty years earlier in the darkest time of my life, but each of us has our own signs of connections with God and other believers. In your own dark moments, remember that God shows up. When the dark night of the soul rises in your life, he is there!

As I write this story, we have been in this house for fifteen years today (August 1, 2017). I spend most of my time outside gardening and fishing. In fifteen years I have never seen a cedar waxwing bird except the three times that grief visited our home. The first sighting was on March 18, 2015, after Bill Thomas passed. The last sighting was exactly one year later, on March 18, 2016, when Lou passed.

When I went to my garden to work, ol' Lou would follow me to the end of the dog run and lie in the corner because that was as close to me as the fence would allow. He wanted to be close and eventually wore out the grass in that corner. Ol' Jack was an outside dog as well. He would lie below the window of Joshua's room because that was as close as he could get. Every night, Jack kept his post below Joshua's window, where the grass faded just like Lou's corner of the yard. The love of those hounds for their masters had worn the grass away. It was as close as they could get.

How close are you to God? How close do you want to be? Are you watching for signs of his closeness? The book of James records a great promise from God: "Draw near to God and he will draw near to you" (James 4:8 NIV). Why are we told to draw near? Because God, like the rock of Gibraltar, never budges from our everyday walk. It is we who tend to wander away in the relationship. Draw as near as you can get, and be ready to experience a positive change, for you will become like him as he takes up his residence in your heart (John 14:15–18 NIV). Now, that is as close as you can get to your Master!

THE REST OF THE STORY

There is a time for everything, and a season for
every activity under heaven: a time to be born and
a time to die, a time to plant and a time to uproot, a
time to weep and a time to laugh, a time to mourn
and a time to dance. (Ecclesiastes 3:1–2, 4 NIV)

It was a typical summer afternoon on our deck overlooking
Boerne Lake. Nancy and I were sipping some cool drinks and
talking about how life happened that day. The big green egg
(large ceramic grill aptly shaped like a big green egg) was heating
up and awaiting some Texas beef. Nancy's cell phone released
its familiar ringtone of banjo music, and she answered. It was
Joshua, and he had news to share. There was no chitchat. Joshua
got to the reason he called right out of the gate. Nancy flashed
her usual big smile and darted her green eyes in my direction.
All her body language was screaming, "Good news!" The call
continued, with Nancy asking the question that explained her
excited nature. "When is the child due to arrive?" At this point,
even I got it. Celeste and Joshua were going to have a baby. It
would be the family's first. When the call ended, Nancy threw
her hands in the air and danced across the deck. She erupted into
a chant like song: "We are going to have a baby. We are going
to have a baby."

It was the best of times in our home in Boerne and in the home of Celeste and Joshua in Chicago.

There is a time for everything under the sun and a season for every activity under heaven. This day on the deck was a day to dance. Celeste and Joshua had been married for six years. Celeste had established a successful career as an architectural designer at large design firms in Dallas and Chicago. Joshua had finished medical school in Fort Worth and was nearing the end of his residency program in Chicago. It was a great time for the family to have its first child. The Pratt family was ready to begin the season of its next generation.

It would be on the same deck about twenty-four weeks later that the season of dancing would yield to a season of mourning. It was a phone call that brought uplifting news, and it would be a phone call that brought deflating news. Joshua called on a Monday evening. He told me that the baby stopped moving on Sunday and they were at the hospital, where the doctors could not find a heartbeat. The ultrasound pictures of baby Pratt came down from the refrigerator, and Nancy boarded a plane to Chicago, leaving Bill and me in Boerne.

It was supposed to be a season of new birth and dancing. The birth-to-death span was supposed to be separated by three score and ten years. Instead, our family went through birth, death, and mourning in a single day. The child was a boy and given the name of Bill Thomas after his uncle and Celeste's grandfather.

The old slave trader turned evangelist John Newton wrote in the 1700s, "Satan can only go to the end of his chain." Today in our family, that chain was too long. What was supposed to be a day of laughter turned into a day of weeping.

When the subject of suffering arises, we often go to the book of Job in the Bible. He was a good man who suffered for no apparent reason. After Job received the news that all ten of his children had perished and all his wealth had been destroyed and he was afflicted with soars from head to toe, he had a brief discourse with his wife:

> His wife said to him, "Are you still holding on to your integrity? Curse God and die!" He replied, "You are talking like a foolish woman. Shall we accept good from God, and not trouble?" In all this, Job did not sin in what he said. (Job 2:9–10 NIV)

What happens when Satan's chain is too long for our comfort? Can we, like Job, be trusted with trouble?

Job did not take the easiest path, but let me illustrate that with a story. My first job after high school was an electrical lineman for the county. Glenn Campbell even wrote a song about me. Well, it was not about me, but it was popular in my day, and I pretended that ol' Glenn was singing about me. I worked at a rural electric cooperative, and Horace Murphey was the journey lineman given the responsibility of taking a scatterbrained boy and teaching him to climb poles. Climbing poles is dangerous work, but it is even more so when thousands of volts of electricity are surging across the tops of those poles. Lesson one from Horace was, "Son, electrons always take the easiest path to the ground." Lesson two from Horace was, "Son, never, never get between electricity on its path to the ground. If you do, there is no chance for survival." We reviewed these two lessons each time before I climbed a pole to help me stay focused on the job. Horace was hard on me because he knew if my mind wandered, it could cost me my life. At the time I did not like Horace's harsh treatment. Today I love Horace Murphey because he loved me enough to drive survival lessons home.

What I am about to say may cause you to close this book if you are presently suffering or have suffered for no apparent reason. Please stay with me. God allows trouble to come our way to help us understand this principle—with God there is always a rest of the story. Few, if any, have suffered as Job did, yet he did not take the easiest path. What would that path be? His wife suggested it: Raise your fist to heaven and curse God for this trouble. Job did not take the easiest path because he believed there was a rest of the story. He did not know that God and Satan had two conversations about his troubles (Job 1–2 NIV). He did not even know if in his lifetime he would see the rest of the story play out (Job 19:25–27 NIV). He just knew there was a rest of the story. He was waiting to discover it. May I encourage you to do the same? Hold on, for heaven is at work building *your* rest of the story.

The rest of our family's story begins with another phone call from Chicago. Joshua called to tell us that he and Celeste were going to have another child. It was only four months since the passing of Bill Thomas. When Nancy had learned of the coming of Bill Thomas, there was dancing on the deck beneath the blue skies of Texas. But all of us had been badly wounded, so the news of a second child was absorbed cautiously. Instead of dancing under the blue skies of Texas, we entered a dimly lit tunnel, not knowing where it would lead.

There was a steady stream of doctor visit reports. All systems were go. Sorry, that is the engineer in me coming out. The big day arrived in the early hours of April 2, 2016. Celeste made it to the hospital, but the doctor did not. The annual Shamrock Shuffle marathon was happening that day, and she was trapped in traffic. A midwife and nurse delivered a boy weighing nine pounds and four ounces and twenty-two inches long. Joshua and Celeste selected the name of Jesse Sullivan. It was a special name, as most names are. Jesse Wilson was Jesse's great-great-great-grandfather, born in Robertson County, Tennessee, in 1882. He was an elder in the church and a farmer. The name Sullivan belonged to the matriarch side of Celeste's family. They too were hardy farmers from the great state of Ohio. Jesse Sullivan's roots go back to tillers of the soil who, in good times and bad, always looked up to God.

Nancy packed her bag for Chicago, and I poked around on the computer for some plane tickets. She would be there to support Celeste and Jesse for their first week at home. Bill and I would stay in Boerne for now, seeking our first opportunity to visit Chicago. As I kissed Nancy goodbye at the security gate, my mind was somewhere between the top of the mountain and the dark valley below the mountain. It had been a year of grief with the loss of a grandson, mother, and sixteen-year-old Labrador. Aged parents and pets are supposed to pass, but a firstborn son should stand at your graveside, not you at his.

Jesse was approaching a birth date, for on June 2 he would be two months old. Our family had been following the Chicago Cubs, who were off to one of their best starts since winning the World Series some 108 years earlier. The Dodgers were playing the Cubs at Wrigley Field on Memorial Day. I called Joshua and suggested that we have a grand celebration by taking Jesse to his first Cubs game, and he quickly agreed. The plan was to secure tickets behind the Cubs' dugout so close that you could clearly hear the baseball strike the catcher's mitt. Joshua executed the plan perfectly. We were close enough to clearly hear the hundred-plus mph fastball pound the mitt and see the unshaven faces of the Cubs batters.

The outing was risky. We had spent hundreds of dollars for tickets hoping that a two-month-old baby could endure nine innings of baseball, including the bus and train rides to the game. It was a risk worth taking. If you are a baseball fan, it does not get much better than a sold-out crowd at Wrigley Field on a blue-sky afternoon in May.

Before the game began, sailors and marines from the base near Chicago unfurled and American flag that covered most of the outfield. The colors were presented at home plate, and we all stood and sang the National Anthem. With new grandson in arms, it was an activity that would consume any bucket list because it would fill the whole bucket in one go.

The risk paid off. Jesse, being the devoted Cubs fan that he is, made it to the ninth inning. Well, truth being told, he slept most of the game. He slept until the final set of outs in the ninth. The Cubs' bull pin closer came in, hurling hundred-plus mph fastballs to strike out those Dodgers and secure a two to zero victory for the Cubs.

Many explanations have been given as to why 2016 was the year for the Cubs to win it all. Cubs' fans had been waiting for 108 years to see the pennant brought back to Chicago. The legendary Cubs radio broadcaster Harry Carry had sung "Take Me out to the Ballgame" season after season in hopes that Cubs fans would be entertained by a winning team rather than his seventh-inning stretch performance. My take on it is that Jesse Sullivan Pratt's attendance on Memorial Day 2016 broke the curse of the goat.

The day before the Dodger/Cubs game, we had lunch at a small Italian restaurant below the elevated rail tracks near downtown Chicago. We went back to Joshua and Celeste's condominium at 1500 West Monroe Street. After a large lunch, some wanted to take a nap. I do not do midafternoon naps very well, so I went for a walk in the neighborhood. Their neighborhood was an interesting place. Chicago fire station for engine-company 103 was beside the condominium, and a few streets over were rows of brownstone Victorian homes.

As I explored the neighborhood, I discovered a market for eclectic items and antiques. The market was a collection of tents surrounding the Plumbers Union Hall a few blocks from West Monroe. I paid a ten-dollar entrance fee, thinking that the market would provide a good hour of entertainment.

There were food vendors selling Chicago hot dogs and other local favorites, but I was still running on full from our Italian feast, so I passed by and went inside the hall to wander among the consignment booths. The offerings in one booth were similar to the offerings of another. I was not looking for anything in particular but remained open to an article that spoke to me on a personal level.

The first article that sparked my interest caused me to haggle over price with the booth attendant. The second article that turned my head produced little back and forth over price because I had to take it home. The first item was a colored pencil sketch of Ronald Regan by artist Elbricke. We as Americans have the right to select the president for which we have the deepest respect. Ronald Regan is high on my list, so the sketch was important to me. The haggling was successful, for that portrait stares back at me as I write this chapter in my home study. The second item was located three booths down on the corner, and it too was a portrait. It was professionally matted in a walnut frame sixteen by twenty inches. I asked the booth attendant where he had obtained the portrait. He explained that he had purchased it from an estate sale at an antebellum home in Virginia. The portrait was signed by the artist J, MOOS, W. and depicted a male and female cedar waxwing birds, the male in the foreground, and the female behind him, perched on a holly branch. She had a holly berry in her mouth, and he struck a defiant pose that displayed well his black mask and blue tail feathers tipped in yellow. The booth attendant closed the deal in record time.

We returned to our home in Boerne on June 2, which marked Jesse's two-month birth date. The first thing I did upon arriving was to secure nail and hammer and a tape measure so I could hang the cedar waxwing portrait. There was no discussion as to where it should hang. It hangs beside the window that overlooks the tree where hundreds of cedar waxwing birds paid us three visits in our year of grief. The first visit came at the passing of Bill Thomas on March 18, 2015. The second visit came on January 3, 2016, when we returned home from Mama Jeannie's graveside service. The third visit came at the passing of our Labrador, Lou, on March 18, 2016.

The portrait of the cedar waxwings hanging by the window is a personal reminder to me that God is near. He is near all the time. Our dining table is beneath the portrait. It is at that table that we laugh and enjoy one another's company. It is at that table that we bow our heads and pray to God. Our son Bill often leads our family in prayer with this opening line, "Come, Lord Jesus, be our guest." We invite Jesus to come join us as if he is absent, but in reality, he is not.

In times of laughter and deep sorrow, God is there with us. He does not change, whereas our circumstances can change with a phone call. The apostle James writes about the nature of God so we will not be deceived:

> "Don't be deceived, my dear brothers. Every good
> and perfect gift is from above, coming down from
> the Father of heavenly lights, who does not change
> like shifting shadows." (James 1:16–17 NIV)

It was a phone call that turned our world upside down with news that our first grandson was stillborn at thirty-two weeks. It was a phone call that gave us cause for celebration and dancing with the news that a healthy nine-pound, four-ounce boy had joined our family. God was there on both occasions and fills the ordinary days with his presence as well. John Lennon states in one of his songs, "Life is what happens to you while you are busy making other plans." We were busy making plans for the arrival of a first grandson, not knowing that the rest of the story would be the need of a funeral director, not a neonatal care unit.

The cedar waxwing portrait hangs by the window every day. It hangs there to remind me that God is an everyday God. He is there in the desperate moments. He is there in the fearful moments of an ordinary day. The prophet Isaiah writes of a God who comes in the fearful moment:

"Say to those with fearful hearts, 'Be strong, and do not fear; your God will come, he will come with vengeance; with divine retribution he will come to save you.'" (Isaiah 35:4 NIV)

Hang on to that promise as life happens. Lennon was right; we cannot plan our way around the circumstances of life. Life is unfolding, and we do what we can to influence the outcome for good. Sometimes the rest of the story is good and we hold our grandson on a blue-sky day at the ballpark, and sometimes the rest of the story brings us to the graveside. God is there as the rest of the story plays itself out.

What about Job's rest of the story? In the first and second chapters of Job, he loses his ten children, his wealth, and his health. He was once a respected man at the city gate and now small boys make fun of him and once-dedicated servants will not answer when he calls out to them. Job was a blameless man according to God.

Then the LORD said to Satan, "Have you considered my servant Job? There is no one on earth like him; he is blameless and upright, a man who fears God and shuns evil" (Job 1:8 NIV)

Job was blameless, but life happens, and for no reason he was afflicted. There are three friends who show up. They are Eliphaz the Temanite, Bildad the Shuhite, and Zophar the Naamathite. They strive to give Job answers that basically boil down to, "Whatever you did wrong, Job, must have been bad for you to be suffering this way." Job had had enough, and he wanted a face-to-face meeting with God. He railed at his friends, "What you know, I also know; I am not inferior to you. But I desire to speak to the Almighty and to argue my case with God" (Job 13:2–3 NIV).

God does not show up until chapter 38, and he does not give Job answers, but rather he asks Job some questions.

> Then the LORD answered Job out of the storm.
> He said: Who is this that darkens my counsel
> with words without knowledge? Brace yourself
> like a man; I will question you and you shall
> answer me. Where were you when I laid the
> earth's foundation? Tell me, if you understand.
> Who marked off the dimensions surely you know!
> (Job 38:1–4 NIV)

God's questions were to show Job that there would be no sass mouth around God. When I was growing up and would talk back to my mama, she would say to me, "Just who do you think you are talking to? Don't you sass me, Daniel Ray Pratt!" God is and will always be sovereign.

For the next two chapters, the Creator speaks to the created. Job begins to see his place in the scheme of things and responds back to God:

> Then Job replied to the LORD: "I know that
> you can do all things; no plan of yours can be
> thwarted. You asked, "Who is this that obscures
> my counsel without knowledge? Surely I spoke of
> things I did not understand, things to wonderful
> for me to know. "You said, "Listen now, and I will
> speak; I will question you and you will answer me.
> My ears had heard of you but now my eyes have
> seen you. Therefore I despise myself and repent
> in dust and ashes." (Job 42:1–6 NIV)

Did you catch the value Job placed on his suffering? Before he suffered, he had heard of God, but the suffering caused him to get a clear picture of God. There is not a good answer for why we suffer. I do know that when I am hurting and go to God, I grow closer to him. This bond grows stronger the next time a life storm strikes me or my family. Maybe God gets lonely for our attention and he allows storms to come our way to draw us closer to him. I know that if my son Joshua forgot about me, I would do something to draw his attention.

The rest of the story for Job was not just getting a clear picture of God and his sovereignty but God sending restoration to Job:

> After Job had prayed for his friends, the LORD made him prosperous again and gave him twice as much as he had before. All his brothers and sisters and everyone who had known him before came and ate with him in his house. They comforted and consoled him over all the trouble the LORD had brought upon him, and each one gave him a piece of silver and a gold ring. The LORD blessed the latter part of Job's life more than the first. He had fourteen thousand sheep, six thousand camels, a thousand yoke of oxen and a thousand donkeys. And he also had seven sons and three daughters. Nowhere in all the land were there found women as beautiful as Job's daughters, and their father granted them an inheritance along with their brothers. After this, Job lived a hundred and forty years; he saw his children and their children to the fourth generation. And so he died, old and full of years. (Job 42:10-17 NIV)

There was another blameless man in the Bible who also suffered unjustly just as Job suffered. He was born into a family steeped in poverty and grew up in a backwater town from where nothing good had come. For the first thirty years of his life, he chose anonymity. Then one day, he appeared at the Jordan River to be baptized by John the Baptist. When John saw him approaching he said, "Behold the lamb of God that takes away the sins of the world!" (John 1:29 NIV).

Jesus stepped onto the stage for the final act of a story that has been playing out since ancient days began in a perfect garden. Our father and mother (Adam and Eve) made wrong choices and stepped outside the boundaries set by God. Sin entered the world, and life has not been fair since that day.

Just as God paid Job a visit, Jesus stepped into our world and for three years walked among us to show us what God is like. Jesus explained his visit as a venture to seek and save that which is lost (Luke 19:10 NIV). Paul tells us in the book of Romans that in reference to the lost, Jesus was speaking about all of us that refuse to participate in his grace. All men have fallen short of God's glory and sinned (Romans 3:23 NIV). He goes on to say that the wages of sin is death, but the gift of God is eternal life in Christ Jesus our Lord (Romans 6:23 NIV). Jesus had come to the earth to be the Lamb of God and offer himself as a sacrifice for our wrongdoing. The just dies for the unjust.

Job had a rest of the story after his suffering, and so did Jesus. The Romans crucified Jesus at the bidding of the religious elite of the day. They wanted Jesus out of the way. He had cut into their money-making business by turning over the money-changers' tables in the temple. Revenues from money changing plunged, and the pious Jews were not going to stand by and see their profit center dwindle. Then there was the matter of his populist appeal. He spoke as one in authority. He spoke as if he *knew* God, not just knew *about* God. He had answers, so the people looked away from the religious elite and toward Jesus. Their eyes were deep green with envy. Jesus suffered death, not just any death, but death on a cruel Roman cross.

The rest of the story for Jesus and our rest of the story as well unfolds on the Emmaus Road three days after the crucifixion (Luke 24:13–35 NIV). Two followers of Jesus are beaten down and returning home from Jerusalem. Their dream was over; Jesus was dead. They had reason to believe that this charismatic teacher and miracle worker would take down the Roman government and restore self-rule to Israel. They had watched the adoring crowd at the triumphant entry into Jerusalem deteriorate into a screaming mob that wanted nothing short of crucifixion. Jesus cried out, "It is finished." With that, he bowed his head and gave up his spirit (John 19:30 NIV).

The hopes and dreams of our Emmaus travelers died that day as well. They walked along the road with downcast faces. Have you ever been there? There is not enough energy or will to hold your head up. The only peace you can find is found by gazing at the ground. As they talked and discussed these things with each other, Jesus himself came up and walked along with them (Luke 24:15 NIV). Jesus has not changed. He still comes alongside in the downcast moments of life to tilt our heads from the downward position to that of looking upward.

Listen to your heart and he will speak into your downcast moment too. He will do it in a way that only you will understand because he is not a distant God but one who is close to the brokenhearted. In my case, he spoke to me personally by sending cedar waxwing birds to visit me on three downcast occasions.

The rooster crows before the dawn. If you have ever been around for that event, you know that the rooster's crow occurs a good hour before the sunrise when the night is at its darkest. Somehow the rooster knows that the sun is about to rise, so he announces it with his crow. In your dark moment, whisper a prayer, and ask that the Son rise in your heart. My friend, you will be changed forever, for there is no friend like Jesus! Remember the words of wise King Solomon: There is a time for everything, and a season for every activity under heaven. Have you had enough discouragement? Could today be your time?

HEY, BILL

> I was young and now I am old, yet I have never seen the righteous forsaken or their children begging bread. (Psalm 37:25 NIV)

This story is being penned at forty thousand feet somewhere over the Pacific. Nancy and I are on a trip we talked about the night we got married some forty years ago. Four hours of an eight-hour flight have passed, and we are halfway between Dallas and Honolulu. With four remaining hours, I took pen in hand to write yet another story of the provision and goodness of God.

All well-run businesses have a vision statement. It is a statement that helps them stay focused through the ebb and flow of profit and loss. When difficult issues seem to sprout like newly sown grass, they use the vision statement to ground them as to what they do and why they do it.

At the beginning of our marriage, Nancy and I did not have a brainstorming session to carefully craft a vision statement for our marriage. For some that might work well, but to us it seemed weird. We do not have a vision statement, but we have always had a vision. I said, "Nancy, someday when our hair is gray, we are going to walk hand in hand down the beach knowing that the passing of time has drawn us closer to one another and closer to our God."

We were young, and now we are old. Where did forty years go, and why is my hair so gray? Lord willing, we will make that walk tomorrow morning when the sun rises and live out a vision that we cast the first night together.

The week leading up to this day has been stressful, with each day becoming more anxiety-filled than the day before. The last check to put in the box before our trip was to take our son Bill to the airport. Bill is a nonreader and excels at sacking groceries at the HEB store in Boerne, Texas. Bill would be flying alone from San Antonio to Atlanta to meet his brother, Joshua, to spend the week.

The anxiety was building because outside of his normal routine, Bill has a tendency to get lost. He got lost riding the elevators in a Madrid hotel. He got lost in a twenty-story hotel in Portugal. He got lost in the Louvre museum in Paris. The boys had a game they played called *Where's Waldo*. It is a familiar game that had an odd little fellow mixed into an eclectic crowd of folks, and the objective was to peer into the crowd and find Waldo. In our family it was not a game, but a real-life adventure. *Where is Bill?* Bill just gets lost. The anxiety before our vacation was rising because for the past thirty-four years, when Bill got lost, we were there to find him. Atlanta is a big airport. Grown men have gone in there to never emerge again.

We worked up a plan A and B for Bill's arrival in Atlanta. We talked Bill through the arrival process on our daily walks, when we ate, and when we got up in the morning and went to bed at night. But Bill has his PhD in slip-sliding away, especially in large crowds.

We followed Paul's advice and lifted up our anxiety to God and prayed with thanksgiving for all those times we were able to find him (Philippians 4:3–7 NIV). The peace that surpasses understanding did not come. Nancy put the issue on the prayer list at her women's Bible study, so we had a bunch of folks praying for a good outcome. We continued to pray right up to the time to go to the airport.

Nancy stayed at home to finish packing, and Bill and I loaded up to go to the airport, where I got a pass to go with Bill to his departure gate. He was tense and unable to be still, so we walked up and down the concourse. Nancy called twice as we walked to go over the plan A and B stuff, and Joshua called as well to give us his travel status en route to the Atlanta airport. Traffic was heavy, and Joshua did not know if he would be there when the plane arrived. Family anxiety continued to bubble up as the departure time drew near.

Boarding time was in ten minutes, so Bill and I made our way to gate A10. As we approached gate A10, the usual preboarding crowd was forming at the Southwest gate. About the time I handed Bill his boarding pass, two women hollered, "Hey, Bill!" They knew Bill as their bagger at HEB. About the time that bit of excitement died down, a man hollered, "Hey, Bill! Who is going to help me carry out my steaks at HEB tonight?" In a ten-minute span, a total of nine people hollered out, "Hey, Bill."

One of them was Patti Nelson, who goes to our church and sits near Bill to enjoy his singing. Being a nonreader, Bill makes a joyful noise if he does not know the song. If he does know the song, brace yourself because the Lord is about to touch your heart. That is especially true if the song is "Victory in Jesus." Many have said that Bill's rendition brings tears to their eyes.

Patti asked about Bill's trip, and when I filled her in on the details, she volunteered to help. She told me she had a two-hour layover in Atlanta, and she would sit with Bill until Joshua arrived. She also gave me her cell number and I gave her Joshua's cell number so we would be sure there was good communication surrounding the Bill exchange. Patti being there and eight more folks who knew Bill on the flight took all the wind out of my anxiety sails.

As Bill and Patti disappeared down the jetway, I called Nancy to give her the "Hey, Bill," times nine report. Nancy's voice broke with emotion as the story unfolded. "God is good," she said.

Earlier in the week when Nancy laid out the prayer request for her Bible study group, Barbara Mooring said, "Don't worry, Nancy. Ol' Bill will see someone who knows him and they will take care of him." When was the last time you got on a plane and about 10 percent of the people on that plane knew you?

There are at least two lessons to draw from, "Hey, Bill." The first is to listen to the saints of God, for he often speaks to you through them. Barbara would have been correct if only Patti Nelson showed up at the gate. But "Hey, Bill," nine times is evidence that God's provision is abundant. He is able to do far more than we can imagine (Ephesians 3:20–21 NIV). The second lesson is more profound: You cannot see what God is doing until you see what God has done. Across the many weeks leading up to the 6:00 p.m. flight from San Antonio to Atlanta, people were making plans. Nine of those people on the flight knew Bill. We had been praying right up until boarding time began, not knowing all the arrangements God was making to give us assurance that His hand was guiding the process. In the ten minutes leading up to the boarding of the plane, it was like all nine of those people were waiting for Bill to show up at the gate. Faith is offering up a prayer, not knowing how God will respond but that he will (Hebrews 11:6 NIV). Heaven is always at work in this world, making arrangements that that we cannot see until those arrangements play out before us and we have an aha moment The Lord is near (Philippians 4:5 NIV).

If your tears are on the church floor, remember that God is at work. You may not be able to see what God has done until tears of joy well up in your eyes as all his behind-the-scenes efforts become visible. God is good all the time.

A HEART THAT GOES OUT

When the Lord saw her, his heart went out to her
and he said, "Don't cry." (Luke 7:13 NIV)

Every morning we go through the same routine. She looks at me
with those big brown eyes, and my heart goes out to her. As I
began this story on a Sunday morning, one of my students from
the Mountain Climbers class raised her hand and said, "Wait a
minute, Dan—your wife Nancy is sitting here beside me, and her
eyes are as green as the grass in the Oklahoma panhandle." The
class begins to reason, *maybe the Sunday school teacher has another
woman in his life.*

"Wait a minute! This is not what it sounds like," I protest.
Those big brown eyes do not belong to another woman. They
belong to our female dachshund named Sister.

As I make my way to the kitchen, Sister is charging ahead
of me. Her whole body is in motion, with all that energy being
channeled down her elongated body to set her tail into a festive
frenzy. My heart always goes out to this pitiful little hound, and
her undivided attention is rewarded with a pinch of bacon from my
breakfast plate. Nancy fusses at me for giving Sister table food. But
I do not mind the scolding because Sister has captured my heart.

What captures your heart? What draws your undivided
attention? There are events that cause you to smile broadly,

and there are events that squeeze your heart and fill your eyes with tears.

A few years ago, my company built a solar power plant near Buckeye, Arizona. My company builds heavy industrial plants from the Carolinas to California. We interact with the local communities in positive ways, always trying to leave a community better than we found it. One such interaction occurred in Buckeye at the elementary school. The students did not have much, so we brought them school supplies, and at Christmastime, we showered them with presents they would have otherwise not received. The children smiled big, and the parents shed tears of joy.

There was the Head Start Program for the children to help them get some educational traction. To show their gratitude, the students in that program made our office a Christmas tree by placing their little hands into green finger paint and then pressing them onto a large white sheet of paper. The outline of their little hands formed a heartwarming impression of a Christmas tree. They wrote thank-you notes and attached them to the tree. One note grabbed my attention and captured my heart. It was written with wobbly letters, and as I studied the note, it occurred to me that it was written upside down and backward. That child was dyslexic and poor. It was a *life is not fair* moment. The child would struggle to keep pace with his peers. His level of effort captured my heart.

What captures the heart of God and draws his undivided attention? There are many Jesus stories in the New Testament that provide insight into this question. Let's examine a couple of stories found in Doctor Luke's seventh chapter.

Jesus traveled to a town called Nain. He was coming from Capernaum, where he had healed the servant of a Roman centurion. The Roman centurion was a man of influence. He commanded one hundred soldiers, and he knew the elders of the Jews. He sent the elders to Jesus, and they pleaded earnestly with Jesus to come to the aid of the centurion's dying servant. Their argument was straightforward: This is a deserving man who loves our nation and he has built a synagogue for us. Jesus followed the elders, and as they approached the centurion's house, he sent out friends to stop Jesus. He had a rare combination of traits in that he was both influential and humble. Claiming that he was not worthy for Jesus to come under his roof, he requested that Jesus simply speak healing words from a distance. Jesus marveled at the faith of the centurion and spoke words of healing. The friends returned to find the servant well.

As Jesus pivoted toward Nain, he heard shouts of praise in the distance. From a distance his heart had gone out to a man of influence to heal his servant. He never saw the centurion or his servant, but his heart was still moved based on his sign of faith.

The disciples and a large crowd were with Jesus as Nain came into view. What if we were part of that crowd following Jesus into Nain? We had just heard shouts of praise rise up out of the centurion's house. We had witnessed healing from a distance through the spoken word. There was no touch, just a word from Jesus. Traveling with Jesus, we had come to expect marvelous, unexplainable events to occur. What miracles awaited us in Nain? What would this day with Jesus bring?

Our crowd intersects another large crowd as we approach the city gate. Our crowd is abuzz with positive energy. Our heads are held high, and we are chattering back and forth as to the day's possibilities. The sounds of sorrow rise up from the crowd coming out of the gate as a coffin comes into view, leading the procession. In the coffin contains a young man, the only son of his mother, and she is a widow. This is her second trip to the graveyard outside of town. She is brokenhearted and crushed in her spirit. Unlike the centurion, she has no influence. She is alone and destined for poverty.

The Psalmist tells us that brokenness always brings God near (Psalm 34:18 NIV). Luke tells us that when Jesus saw her, his heart went out to her, and he said, "Don't cry." In that dry, dusty moment when all seems lost, the heart of God reaches into the lonely world of a widow. Jesus steps forward and touches the coffin, and the processions stops. There will be no long-distance healing in this case as Jesus commands, "Young man, I say to you, get up!" The young man follows Jesus's commands, and he sits up and begins to talk. Jesus helps him down and gives him back to his mother. Her tears of grief are replaced by inexpressible joy. Can you imagine what was said around their supper table that night? They experienced resurrection and reunion all in the same day. Wow, what a party they must have had.

Two crowds intersect each other at the city gate. One is led by Jesus and is abuzz with the sounds of excitement fueled by anticipation. The other crowd is led by a coffin with the sounds of sorrow hovering overhead. When Jesus gave the command to sit up and the young man did so, both crowds merged into one with awe and praises for God. The crowd concludes that God has come to help his people. That scene at the gate of Nain occurred two thousand years ago, but nothing has changed, for God still comes to help his people.

A special collection of God's people within the Oak Hills Church are the Mountain Climbers class. The class is comprised of older folks who have been followers of Christ since Eisenhower's first term as president of the United States. Over this span of years, they have shed tears of joy and sorrow on the church house floor. They have taken all that life can throw at them, and they remain faithful to God and each other.

Janet is a member of our Mountain Climbers class. She has been and continues to be a great servant in God's kingdom. While in college she went to Cuba to minister to young people. It was a dangerous time as a fellow named Castro was in the mountains stirring up revolution. He continued to stir up trouble, and Janet returned to the States, where she married a delightful young man named Jerry. Both had hearts for Christ. They spent four years in the Philippines as missionaries. Janet returned to the

States once again to take a position with the Salvation Army, where she worked for many years. During those years, she and Jerry managed to have two children: a boy named Jeff and a girl named Jill.

Life was good for Jerry and Janet. The children were grown and married, and Janet continued her work with the Salvation Army, while Jerry was a professor at the college near their Michigan home. Jill had a son and two daughters who were twins but not identical twins. Being grandparents and making meaningful contributions at their workplace suited Jerry and Janet.

Jill's life was fulfilling but draining. Chasing a three-year-old around the house is an endurance test for even a young mother, but multiply those efforts by two and even the heartiest would have to catch a breath. The shortness of breath was at first chalked up to the boundless energy of the twins, but it was soon accompanied by dizziness and chest pain. The young twenty-three-year-old mother decided to visit the doctor.

Jill's test revealed that she had pulmonary arterial hypertension (PAH), which is a rare lung disease that strikes one in one hundred thousand young adults. A three-year fight against the disease ensued and ended with the passing of a twenty-six-year-old mother with six-year-old twins, a son, and a husband left to sort out life without her. A year after Jill passed, the family took another blow when they learned that one of the twins was afflicted with PAH. Her struggle lasted eleven years before she joined her mama.

Janet told me that after Jill's death she returned to her work at the Salvation Army. She parked in her parking spot and got out of the car to resume her duties in the office. Janet said, "I reached down to open the door and just froze. 'How can I open this door and walk into the office as I have done for years? This is not a normal day.' I would be facing a new normal. I appealed to God, 'Lord, you are going to have to help me.' The verse from Job came to me, 'Though he slay me, yet will I hope in him.' In that moment, I became Job. I was a blameless missionary for years and had always served God as best I could. Like Job, my child was gone. I was facing a new normal, as he did. The power I needed to open that door and carry on was available to me if I followed Job's example. I was determined that no matter what came at me, I would not turn away from God, but go deeper into an inexhaustible ocean of faith in him. With Job-like faith, I opened the door and stepped into a new normal."

Social lines are snapped in two when the heart of God goes out. Whether one is an influential commander in the Roman army or a poor, grieving widow at the city gate, God's heart goes out. It goes out, moved by faith or compassion. When your tears fall to the church house floor, each one is recorded in heaven, for your pain matters to a God whose heart always goes out to help his people. It makes no difference who you are; if you are facing a new normal, face it with a God who cares and has promised, "Never will I leave you, Never will I forsake you" (Hebrews 13:5 NIV).

LET NO ONE LOSE HEART

David said to Saul, "Let no one lose heart on account of this Philistine; your servant will go and fight him." (1 Samuel 17:32 NIV)

We were young and had nothing of value using worldly standards of measure. Our bank accounts were thin. If we did make a purchase, it had to be calculated beforehand. We each shared a dorm room with two roommates. We were in college, where few had money or possessions.

By the world's standards, we had little. According to the Beatles, we had what money could not buy—love. Our dates were simple affairs: we would pick up a couple of hamburgers at Hardy's and a package of Kool-Aid at the 7-Eleven. We would then find a quiet spot on the Stones River and feast on hamburgers and share a magnum of Kool-Aid. After our feast, Nancy would take up a position on a rock overlooking the river and watch me fly fish. I often lose myself when I fly fish, and she soon would become bored from lack of attention and drift off to sleep. By the world's standards, we had nothing, but our hearts were open to one another, so we considered ourselves rich.

Have you ever gone without? Do you remember your lean times as some of the best times? Examine the heart for the answer to these questions. The heart was open to God's riches instead of the world's. When a person has an open heart toward God, he always fills it. Incredible things begin to happen when we have nothing more valuable than our relationship with God.

There was a time when the least son of Jesse had nothing. His important brothers were in service to King Saul and involved in the vital business of homeland security. David was too young to be of value to the army of Israel. He was an errand boy dispatched by his father to take grain, bread, and cheese to his elder brothers and return with news of their well-being to ease the mind of a loving father.

David reached the camp just as the army was moving out to the battle lines. The lines were formed across the valley of Elah. The Philistines occupied one hill and the army of Israel the other. David made a quick stop at the supply sergeant's tent and then searched for his brothers in the ranks. About the time David was giving his brothers a high five, the Philistine lines parted, and their prized giant started his daily routine. Each morning the army of Israel would form battle lines and give a war cry and then freeze in their tracks, terrified by the giant Goliath from Gath. Each morning Goliath emerged from the line and shouted with defiance to the army of Israel, and they would turn and run. It was like a scene from the movie *Groundhog Day*, where the groundhog always sees his shadow and retreats.

Before we come down hard on the front-line foot soldiers of Israel, let's step into their sandals. Goliath was over nine feet tall. If he were in the NBA, he could dunk the ball standing flat-footed. He was incredibly strong, as his scaled armor weighed 125 pounds. He would have been a man's man in the weight room of the Green Bay Packers. He wore a helmet of bronze, his legs were fitted with bronze greaves, and across his back was a bronze javelin that weighed fifteen pounds. In my mind I see an ugly man with twisted facial features and breath bad enough to stop the charge of a moose. Each day the rank and file heard the same offer from the giant:

"Why do you come out and line up for battle?
Am I not a Philistine, and are you not the
servants of Saul? Choose a man and have him
come down to me. If he is able to fight and
kill me, we will become your subjects; but if I
overcome him and kill him, you will become our
servants and serve us. This day I defy the ranks
of Israel! Give me a man and let us fight each
other." (1 Samuel 17:8–10 NIV)

There were no takers against such overwhelming odds.
Each man was terrified of the outcome, for surely Goliath was
invincible. Saul especially was terrified since he was a head taller
than his entire army and the mostly likely candidate to take on
Goliath.

This scene was repeated for thirty-nine days, and on the
fortieth day, David showed up to hear the defiant Goliath's offer.
David asked the men in the ranks, "What will be done for the
man who kills this Philistine and removes this disgrace from
Israel? Who is this uncircumcised Philistine that he should defy
the armies of the living God?" (1 Samuel 17:26 NIV). They
explained that the man who took out Goliath would be given
great wealth by the king. The king would also give his daughter
to the man and exempt his father's family from taxes.

Eliab, David's oldest brother, overheard the conversation and
burned with anger. Going on the attack, Eliab interrupted: "Why
have you come down here? And with whom did you leave those
few sheep in the desert? I know how conceited you are and how
wicked your heart is; you came down only to watch the battle" (1
Samuel 17:28 NIV). Ask yourself: why did Eliab become angry?
Could it be that David's heart exposed his own cowering heart?
Eliab was the one with a heart problem, not David. Eliab and all
of Israel had stood in shame on the sidelines for thirty-nine days.
They approached the challenge of Goliath with conventional

89

wisdom, while David approached Goliath with an open heart to God and his provisions.

Saul was informed of the bold statements made by a confident David, so he sent for him. The army of Israel and their leader, Saul, had spent the last thirty-nine days in a loop-de-loop of fear. Each day they were reminded of the failures of the day before. They were beaten down. They had a bad case of the drops-in-heart trouble. They had dropped down and just did not have the heart to get up and go. Imagine the boldness of David when he entered Saul's presence and proclaimed, "Let no one lose heart on account of this Philistine; your servant will go and fight him!"

Saul quickly discounted David: "You are just a boy and Goliath has been a killing machine since his youth." Eliab and Saul saw David as the scrawny shepherd boy that he was, and by earthly standards they were right. David couldn't follow through with his bold claims. They were correct that in David's strength, he was but dust in the wind. David's view of the situation was quite different. He was not a nobody. He was not just an errand boy. He was not just a shepherd boy tending a few sheep in the desert. His heart was open to God and the provisions that David knew would come if only he stepped out in faith. David rebutted the king with, "Let me tell you about the lion and the bear that came against my flock and how God delivered them into my hands." David spoke out of confidence that God would show up just as he had always done in the past.

My work takes me to Old Ocean, Texas, where we are building a massive chemical complex for one of the largest chemical companies in the country. The route I travel is one that cuts across South Texas on State Highway 111. Highway 111 is a scenic route with cattle and grain on top of the ground and the Eagle Ford shale beneath it. The land is flat and the highway straight. I think that the survey team that laid out Highway 111 used a 30-6 rifle. They fired a shot straight down range, and where that shot landed, they fired another. All is visible down Highway 111. Life in a fallen world is not that way. There are many turns along the way that that cause us to pause and think, *I can't carry on.* Where do you get the heart to carry on? When you open your heart to God, expect it to be filled. If you want to gain heart, then you must give it away. In the world's economy, you do not gain by giving things up, but in God's economy, you certainly do. David gave his heart to God and trusted God to show up—and he did exactly that. Want to become fearless against the naysayers? Do you want to charge against that giant that continues to drain your heart's energy? Do you want to become part of the "I can" movement? Give your heart to trusting God. He has said, "Never will I leave you never will I forsake you" (Hebrews 13:5 NIV). That applied to David as he picked up five smooth stones and charged his giant, and it will apply to you as you charge yours.

Never will I leave you or forsake you applied to Greg Pruett and his family. Greg was trained as an engineer, but his heart was pulled not by the thrill of designing and building systems to benefit man but by the incredible message of the love God has for man. Greg dedicated himself to translating the Bible into the Yalunka language, which is a language spoken in Africa by a quarter million people. Greg and his family left their familiar surroundings in Texas and went to Africa to live and work with the Yalunka people. It took twelve years to first learn the language, then translate the Bible into that language. One night at the Oak Hills Church in San Antonio, Texas, Greg stood and held up a thumb drive, declaring the work finished. Only Satan knows how many times he made a run at Greg with the *you can't possibly do this* message. *Give up, go home. You have been at it for a year and look what pitiful progress has been made.* Year after year Satan came back, trying to bring Greg down. But Greg did not lose heart because he had given his to God to use as he saw fit. In time the devil stopped coming by because Greg was a waste of his time since the heart of the matter was already in the ever-present hands of God.

Never will I leave you never will I forsake you applied to the first elders of the Oak Hills church. They were four men who left the security of a larger church in San Antonio to start a mission effort on the outskirts of town. They met and prayed together, and I am sure the devil whispered doubt in their ears plenty of times. As each man reached for the pen to sign a mortgage note to buy land and build a church, that old serpent hissed, "You are taking a serious risk to your family's finances." They did not lose heart because they had given their hearts to the God who never forsakes.

My friend Max Lucado has written scores of books about Jesus. He is an author known across the world for his unique way of expressing the love of God for us and relating our everyday lives to the message of Christ crucified. When Max wrote the first paragraph of the first manuscript, the old serpent hissed, "You can't possibly make a difference. Who are you? Why you are an unknown errand boy trying to deliver a message the world cares little to hear." Max, like Greg and the Oak Hills elders, did not lose heart because he had entrusted it to God, who can do all we ask or can even imagine (Ephesians 3:20 NIV).

As David approached Goliath, he armed himself with five smooth stones from the valley floor and moved to face the giant. Goliath looked him over and saw that he was just a boy, ruddy and handsome, and he despised him. Goliath roared, "Am I a dog that you come at me with sticks?" The giant cursed David by his gods. "Come here," he said, "and I'll give your flesh to the buzzards."

David fired back, "You come at me with sword and spear, but I come at you in the name of the Lord Almighty, the God of the armies of Israel whom you have defiled. Today Goliath you will be buzzard bait, and all will know there is a God in Israel."

The rest of the army of Israel saw a giant too big to bring down, whereas David saw a target too big to miss because God would direct the smooth stone to the forehead of Goliath. With a muffled thud, it struck its target. The next sound on that ancient battlefield was the crash of Goliath's nine-foot frame on to the dusty floor of the valley of Elah. When you take heart by giving your heart to God, then giants fall. What giant are you facing? Send up an SOS prayer and trust God to never forsake you, and then move out. Fear paralyzed King Saul and the army of Israel because they saw a foe that, if met on his terms, would mean certain defeat. Faith freed David as he reset the terms with God in the equation. You can do the same! Pray and move out. God will make a way. He is in the "Make a Way" business.

Let's pick up another story of David. Once again, Israel was battling the Philistines. Once again, the people of Gath were involved. Once again, the army faced giants. Let's pick up the action in 1 Chronicles 20. Elhanan son of Jair killed Lahmi the brother of Goliath the Gittite, who had a spear with a shaft like a weaver's rod. In still another battle, which took place at Gath, there was a huge man with six fingers on each hand and six toes on each foot—twenty-four in all. He also was descended from Rapha. When he taunted Israel, Jonathan son of Shimea, David's brother, killed him (1 Chronicles 20:5–6 NIV). Many years had passed, and the Philistines remained a powerful threat to Israel.

The young shepherd boy was now an accomplished King. The army of Israel reported to King David. He called for his top general, Joab, and the commanders of the army. He ordered them to count the Israelites from Beersheba to Dan and report back to him the number of troops in his army. Joab was a veteran who had been at David's side through many campaigns and had witnessed the hand of God working for Israel. Joab protested and told David, "Has not God always multiplied our troops to get the job done?" Trusting his own might, David overruled him, so Joab went through the land taking a census of the fighting men. Joab reported back that there were one million, one hundred thousand men who could handle a sword.

Joab was a good soldier and followed his orders, but he was repulsed by David's arrogance. The old serpent hissed in David's ear, "You can't go into battle without knowing the size of your army." David followed through with the deceiver's temptation and turned to his own strength instead of placing trust in God. It was the disgust of a trusted friend that opened the eyes of David to his sin. David's heart was swayed by Satan, and it began to calculate using self as the common denominator instead of God. God provided a way out through the accountability of a trusted friend. He may be doing the same for you as you face your giant. If a friend has pointed you away from self and toward God, listen and give your heart back to God. It worked for an old king, and it will for you as well.

A shepherd boy stepped into the presence of a king and declared, "Let no one lose heart." His confidence came from a deep faith in God to always be at his side. He gained heart by giving it away. One day a teacher of the law approached Jesus with a burning question. "Teacher, there are many laws to follow; please tell me the most important one."

"The most important one," answered Jesus, "is this: 'Hear O Israel, the Lord our God the Lord is one. Love the Lord your God with all your heart and with all your soul and with all your mind and with all your strength!'"

"Grow still before the Lord and know He is God" (Psalm 46:10 NIV). The stillness will be interrupted shortly by the thud of a lifeless giant in your own valley of Elan. Look well to this day, and hold back nothing!

THE CALL OF THE MORNING STAR

"Come to me, all you who are weary and
burdened, and I will give you rest. Take my yoke
upon you and learn from me, for I am gentle and
humble in heart, and you will find rest for your
souls. For my yoke is easy and my burden is light."
(Matthew 11:28–30 NIV)

My great-grandmother, Jenny Jennings, was a mail-order
bride. She was born and raised in Ripley, Tennessee, which
is on the banks of the mighty Mississippi River. Jenny placed an
advertisement in a newspaper that made its way to Robertson
County, Tennessee, where a young sharecrop farmer read about
her with interest. Jesse Wilson responded to the advertisement,
which began a letter-writing campaign between the twenty-one-
year-old Jenny and nineteen-year-old Jesse. The letter-writing
campaign ended when Jesse got on a train to West Tennessee
and met Jenny for the first time. They married in Springfield,
Tennessee, in 1901.

Their union would last a lifetime, as Jesse would die in
his sleep at the ripe old age of eighty-two in the home that he
and Jenny built together. They raised four children and two
grandchildren in that white frame farmhouse. The house set at
the top of a hill overlooking a graveled county road. Visiting the

farmhouse and all of its features was like having your own natural history museum.

One feature that drew my attention as a six-year-old was the dinner bell located at the edge of Grandma Jenny's flower garden and beside the cistern. There were many boundaries set for me when I explored the farm, especially two boundaries that I was to never cross. One was playing around the cistern. Grandma Jenny did not want me throwing things into their water supply or positioning myself for a long fall down. The second boundary was ringing the dinner bell.

The dinner bell was the 911 of life on the farm in the early 1900s. If there was trouble on your place, you would ring the bell continuously. A bell that rang out across the community in that manner meant either that there was trouble on your farm or that the preacher was calling folks to church on Sunday morning.

The main use of the dinner bell was to call Jesse and the field hands out of the field and to the dinner table. When Jenny and Jesse started farming in the early 1900s, they used mules to work the ground. When the team of mules heard the dinner bell, they would break into a steady trot back to the barn for some grain and water, and then Jesse and the hands would wash up for dinner. The mules and men came running when Jenny rang the dinner bell because it was a clear signal that they were in for a feast and some rest.

Jesse and the men would gather around the table as steam rose up from the bowls of potatoes, beans, and freshly sliced cornbread. Jesse would bow his head and pray. One could tell that Jesse talked to God often. His voice had a reverence that could be felt. After dinner was over, Jenny would lay her head down on folded hands and rest before clearing the table and cleaning the kitchen. Meanwhile, Jesse and the men would take their rest in the shade of the maple trees in the front yard.

Six days a week, the call to dinner was indicated by the clear sound of the dinner bell. The bell always had the same clear tone each time it rang, and it rang with integrity. It was a call to a feast and some needed rest.

The call issued by Jesus has integrity. Jesus said, "Come to me, all you who are weary and burdened, and I will give you rest." The call does not change like the shifting of shadows in the late afternoon. Have you ever been up before dawn? I prefer to do my writing in the early hours of the morning, and when I look out over Boerne Lake, I can see the morning star rising on the eastern horizon. It casts a pale blue light onto the surface of the lake. The presence of the morning star does not change. If the sky is clear, then the shaft of pale blue light is visible. Clouds may block the light from the lake's surface, but it is still there, even if it is out of sight.

The call of Jesus for me to come to Him is as consistent and unchanging as the rising of the morning star. Perhaps, though, the circumstances in our lives may be so inflamed that we cannot hear the call of Jesus to rest. When we are too focused on our own agenda, or as I like to call it, in "me mode," we can be distracted from his call.

Nancy and I were out for our morning walk one day, down by the edge of the lake. It was a peaceful morning with a chorus of doves calling from the cedar trees. The lake had a mirror finish that glimmered like a pool of mercury when the sun peeked over the Texas hills: It was definitely going to be a blue-sky day. All the beauty of the morning passed over my head, though, because I was in me mode. Have you ever been there? We have an affinity for me mode. We take to it like a duck to water, and nothing seems to go in our favor when we pitch our tent in me mode camp. Complaints are spewing from our mouths like shots from a roman candle on the Fourth of July.

Nancy listened to me carry on for a few minutes without responding. I cannot remember what I was upset about, but I do remember how she eventually threw a bucket of water on my me mode rant. Nancy flared those green eyes at me and said, "Dan Pratt, you need to grow still and know that He is God." Or as the Psalmist writes, "Be still, and know that I am God."

When you are in me mode, the only help available is self-help. If you step out of your bubble of self-interest and grow still before God, there is rest from the burden that causes our weariness. The Psalmist, again from Psalm 46, makes this uplifting promise:

> God is our refuge and strength, an ever present help in trouble. Therefore we will not fear, though the earth give way and the mountains fall into the sea, though its waters roar and foam and the mountains quake with their surging. (Psalm 46:1–3 NIV)

When we are in me mode, fear multiplies like bacteria in a petri dish. When we are in me mode, circumstances overwhelm us like the roaring water of the sea erase a sandcastle. We need a sea wall upon which we can rest, safe from the waves. Jesus says, "Let me be that wall. Come learn of me, for I am meek and lowly in heart and you will find rest for your souls." The rest offered by Jesus penetrates deeper than muscle and sinew to push worries from the heart. Paul speaks of this rest from Jesus as a peace that surpasses understanding:

> Rejoice in the Lord always. I will say it again: Rejoice! Let your gentleness be evident to all. The LORD is near. Do not be anxious about anything, but in everything, by prayer and petition, with thanksgiving, present your request to God. And the peace of God, which transcends all understanding, will guard your hearts and minds in Christ Jesus. (Philippians 4:4–7 NIV)

There is story in the Bible about a me mode moment for a friend of Jesus named Martha. Martha and her sister, Mary, lived in the village of Bethany, which was about six miles from Jerusalem. Whenever Jesus was in that neck of the woods, he would often visit their home.

On one such occasion, Mary was resting at the feet of Jesus to refresh her soul. Meanwhile, Martha was in the kitchen making biscuits. At first Martha gently kneaded the dough, adding flour and buttermilk as needed. However, as all the task of preparing the meal built up in her head, she began to knead the dough faster and faster. Martha pondered, "Where is Mary when there is so much to be done?" She could hear the conversation between Jesus and Mary in the adjoining room, and she began a spiral down into me mode. The color of her face moved from pink to a light shade of red, and a swirl of her hair broke from behind her head to hang beside her nose. She wiped the beads of sweat from her forehead, leaving behind a smudge of flour. Martha's me moment peaked, and she said, "Lord, don't you care that my sister has left me to do all the work by myself? Tell her to help me!"

The pressure control value for her emotions found its release. She had given the Lord a command and used an exclamation point to punctuate it. How did Jesus respond to Martha's outburst, though? "'Martha, Martha,' the Lord answered, 'You are worried and upset about many things, but only one thing is needed. Mary has chosen what is better, and it will not be taken away from her'" (Luke 10:41–42 NIV). Notice there are no exclamation points to punctuate the words of Jesus, because he spoke into the situation with gentleness and deep understanding of Martha's frenzied fit.

Martha had passed from the state of hustling to get things done to the state of hurrying to get things done. The state of hurry causes you to grit your teeth and blow your car horn when delayed. The state of hurry causes you to raise your voice and bark out commands when the family is slow to assemble for a time-sensitive event. Time was a commodity that both Martha and Mary processed in different ways. Mary had prioritized her time well by first spending time with Jesus. Martha had missed that step and went from hustling through activities, to hurrying through activities, then into melting down as time slipped away.

Thankfully, Nancy recognized me going into me mode and snapped me out of my downward spiral by telling me to be like Mary and not like Martha. When we lived in southern Spain, I would leave our house about three hours before daylight and drive north to Madrid. The first leg of the journey was along winding roads through the mountains to Sevilla. The slow pace would bring out the Martha side of me. The more I tried to hurry, the less progress I seemed to make.

By the time I got to the plains outside of Madrid, the sun was rising. The highway to Madrid was a flat ribbon of concrete cutting across vast fields of sunflowers. It was as if Moses had raised his staff and parted the sunflower field, allowing me to drive through with a wall of sunflowers on each side. Each sunflower assumed the same posture: They leaned slightly to the east to take in the nourishing rays of the sun. Through the process of photosynthesis, the sunflowers use the energy from the sun to manufacture the nutrients that sustain life. Mary was like the sunflowers because she was leaning into Jesus that she might get the energy for her life.

The call of Jesus to come to him is constant and consistent. It is a call issued to everyone, a universal call, because we all need rest. The call is often hard to hear because of the noise in our lives. There are always kids to drop off and pick up so they can make their next event. There is always the sound of the Monday-morning alarm calling us to another demanding week. There is the deadline coming next week that sucks the life out of the weekend. These are all time-related situations that cause us to hurry. Then there is the health issue that looms over us, causing us to not hurry, but to worry.

Dear child of God, cling to this promise from Jesus:

> "Here I am! I stand at the door and knock. If anyone hears my voice and opens the door, I will come in and eat with him, and he with me." (Revelation 3:20 NIV)

We can do more by doing less if we open the door and let him into our hearts. Be like a sunflower on the plains outside Madrid, and lean into the Son.

DO MORE BY DOING LESS

I have been crucified with Christ and I no longer live, but Christ lives in me. The life I live in the body, I live by faith in the son of God, who loved me and gave himself for me. (Galatians 2:20 NIV)

When I was a young lad, money was constantly in short supply at home. But that did not stop me from dreaming. I had my eye on a Daisy BB gun at Woodard Hardware Store, which was located across the street from the Springfield Courthouse. The price tag on the Daisy BB gun read twelve dollars. This was equivalent to twelve weeks of wages, as I sold the *Robertson County Times* each week for ten cents a copy. My business model was to buy twenty copies of the *Times* from the owner of the newspaper, Mr. Berlin Clinard, each Wednesday for a nickel each, and sell them for a dime. In the span of two hours, I would double my money, and I never failed to sell all of my papers. At ten years of age, I had discovered a perpetual money-making process. I was young and now I am old, and I have never had a job as rewarding.

Mr. Paul Spec, the owner of Woodard Hardware, knew of my affinity for the Daisy BB gun, so I struck a deal with Mr. Paul. Each week for twelve weeks, I would pay him a dollar until the debt was paid. Every Wednesday after school, I would give Mr. Berlin my dollar and take my papers to the corner of Fifth

Avenue and Walnut and wait for the four o'clock whistle to blow at the Wilson Plant. As the folks left the Wilson Plant, I would hustle up and down the street exchanging newspapers for dimes.

When my papers sold out, I went to visit Mr. Paul at the hardware store. It became a Wednesday-afternoon ritual at Woodard's hardware. This overweight kid, fattened by his mama's biscuits, would rush through the front door and head to the cash register at the back of the store. Mr. Paul would say, "Dan, did you sell all your papers?" The crowd around the warm morning stove would lean forward for the answer. With a pocket full of dimes and a smile on my face, I blurted out, "Yes sir, Mr. Paul, and I have come to pay my debt."

Mr. Paul gave me the Daisy BB gun when I gave him my first dollar. I had a Daisy BB gun with no BBs for twelve weeks. Each week I kept a dollar in reserve to buy the next week's papers. On week thirteen, I bought BBs and life was good. Mr. Paul and I had struck a deal and sealed it with a handshake. We each lived up to the terms and conditions. For his part, Mr. Paul got a kick out of seeing this chubby kid come into the store each week to pay his bill. As for me, I worked hard and followed the rules set out in the agreement with Mr. Paul; it was an agreement that depended on my performance. I would follow these same principles to buy cars and houses later in my life, with far less fanfare and joy. But what about the debt that is unpayable, regardless of my performance?

When Jesus walked on earth, the most religious men of the day were called Pharisees. They set out to strictly keep the law of God. They had taken the Ten Commandments and expanded them to include some 612 regulations that they called the law. The apostle Paul was a Pharisee who dedicated himself to keeping all of the regulations prescribed by his religious sect. Paul's commitment was not just for twelve weeks but was a lifetime commitment. The load that the Pharisees were requiring men to carry was to keep all the regulations all the time: if you broke one rule, it was game over.

The Pharisees were powered by self and not by God. They would lay harsh requirements on themselves and on their fellow man, creating a success principle that depended upon man's efforts. It was a formula that yielded frustration and a constant sense of failure. They had made hypocrisy into an art form. What you saw on the outside mattered the most.

There is a story in the Old Testament about the selection of a king to rule Israel. The people wanted a king so they would be like all the other peoples of the time. God was against the idea and told them that taxes and military service would be heavy burdens to bear, but they would not listen and continued to ask for a king. Eventually God gave them what they wanted.

> There was a Benjamite, a man of standing, whose name was Kish son of Abiel, the son of Zeror, the son of Becorath, the son of Aphiah of Benjamin. He had a son named Saul, an impressive young man without equal among the Israelites- a head taller than any of the others. (1 Samuel 9:1–2 NIV)

Saul, from all appearances, seemed to be a perfect fit. There is a problem with Saul, though. The problem was not visible because Saul was a man with deep-seated pride issues. He refused to follow instructions, and God eventually removed him as king and instructed Samuel to anoint a second king.

Samuel was instructed to go visit with Jesse, for out of the stump of Jesse from the tribe of Judah would come the next king of Israel. Samuel visited with Jesse and stated his business. Jesse had eight sons, and he started to present them to Samuel one by one, starting with the oldest son, Eliab.

> When Samuel arrived and saw Jesse's oldest son Eliab he thought, "Surely the LORD's anointed stands here before the LORD." But the LORD

said to Samuel, "Do not consider his appearance
or his height, for I have rejected him. The LORD
does not look at the things man looks at. Man
looks at the outward appearance but the LORD
looks at the heart." (1 Samuel 16:6–7 NIV)

After bringing seven sons forward to Samuel and having each
one rejected by God, Samuel asked Jesse, "Are these all the sons
that you have?"

"There is still the youngest son," Jesse answered, "but he is
tending the sheep."

Samuel instructed that the youngest son, David, be brought
to him. When David arrived, the Lord instructed Samuel to arise
and anoint David as king of Israel. From that day forward, the
Spirit of the Lord came upon David in power.

Notice David's power source: it was not him, but the power
of God's Spirit working through him, that created the energy for
success.

Saul and his fellow Pharisees looked good from the outside,
but inside there were big problems. Jesus encountered many groups
of people in his time on earth. He dealt with the Romans, harlots,
tax collectors, and drunkards, but no group drew his wrath like
the Pharisees. Matthew 23 has seven woes cast at the Pharisees,
and the following statements of Jesus vividly demonstrate the
hypocrisy of the religious elite of his day:

"Woe to you, teachers of the law and Pharisees,
you hypocrites! You clean the outside of the cup
and dish, but inside they are full of greed and
self-indulgence. Blind Pharisee! First clean the
inside of the cup and dish, and then the outside
also will be clean. Woe to you, teachers of the
law and Pharisees, you hypocrites! You are like
whitewashed tombs, which look beautiful on

the outside but on the inside are full dead men's bones and everything unclean. In the same way, on the outside you appear to people as righteous but on the inside you are full of hypocrisy and wickedness." (Matthew 23:25–28 NIV)

Along comes Jesus, and he changes the rules such that we not only have a chance at success but a guaranteed place in the victor's circle. He makes a promise not for us to do more or work harder, though. His promise is dependent on what he has done for us and is noticeably void of what we have accomplished. His promise goes out to all the frustrated would-be keepers of the law. Listen to his promise from John's account:

"If you love me, you will obey what I command. And I will ask the Father, and he will give you another Counselor and he will be with you forever- the Spirit of truth. The world cannot accept him, because it neither sees him or knows him. But you know him, for he lives with you and will be in you. I will not leave you as orphans; I will come to you." (John 14:15–18 NIV)

Please follow along for another story. It is a story about one of my fellow elders at the Oak Hills Church. His name is Jim Barker, and he is one of the best Bible teachers I have ever heard. Sit at Jim's feet for a while, and you get the impression that he has had face-to-face conversations with the apostle Paul. But Jim has not always walked close to Christ. Rather, this is a story about doing more by doing less.

Jim was good enough at the game of golf to earn his living through the playing and teaching of the game. Several years ago, Jim was on the PGA tour. In his early days on the PGA tour, Jim had little time or appreciation for Christians. He enjoyed playing and beating Christians at golf. When he won the game, he would say to his Christian opponent, "Lions one, Christians zero."

Then one day he crossed a line that he thought he would never cross: he cheated at golf. He was playing in the Texas Open and hit a drive off of the tee that rolled to a dead stop less than a foot out of bounds. When Jim approached his ball and saw that it was inches from being in bounds, he gave the ball a little nudge with his foot. He avoided the out of bounds penalty without being detected. The outside of his cup appeared clean, but on the inside a dark stain formed.

The next day, Jim went for a long run. He could not shake the feeling of guilt that lingered from his actions on the golf course the day before. He had done the unthinkable. Finally, as the weight became unbearable, Jim fell to his knees and cried out to Christ, "Lord, come into my meaningless life, and restore my vigor for living." The Lord always comes when the sincere heart calls out. Jim told us, "From that day forward to this day, Jesus has been working inside of me to form me into his likeness."

When Jim shared his testimony in front of the Oak Hills Church, he had the stage attendants bring a simple table to him at the center of the stage. Jim placed a large clear pitcher on the table and filled it half full of crystal-clear water. Jim suspended a large tea bag in the clear water and continued to talk about the influence of Christ working on him from the inside. Jim spoke of the fruit of the Spirit, which is love, joy, peace, patience, goodness, gentleness, kindness, faithfulness, and self-control. As he spoke, the clear water was slowly being stained a deep brown color by the tea. Jesus works from the inside to make real positive change take place. He cleans out all the hypocrisy. The power of Jim's example was all the water that became stained by the tea; every molecule was changed. The Spirit's desire is to change us in the very same way.

We do more by doing less when we release and let the Spirit drive change in our life. I have heard people pray in a public setting for God to send us more of his Spirit that we might be full of his Spirit. The issue is not God sending His Spirit with greater intensity but in our willingness to release our hold on all the aspects of our life and allow the Spirit to penetrate. The problem is self; it gets in the way of us having the fruit of the Spirit multiplying in our lives.

The zealot Saul started his journey to becoming the apostle Paul on the road to Damascus, where he witnessed the risen Christ. Saul left Jerusalem full of self. He would not return to Jerusalem for many years, and when he did, he was completely changed. He left Damascus under the cover of darkness by being let down the city's wall in a basket. He would flee to Arabia, where for three years the Spirit peeled away all the layers that made up Saul until self was gone. It was in that wilderness that Paul began to realize he must do more by doing less, by allowing God's Spirit to influence his every thought. Saul became Paul not in Damascus but as the Spirit stained his life in the loneliness of the wilderness.

Listen to Saul who became Paul: "I have been crucified with Christ. It is no longer I that live but Christ who lives in me. The life I now live I live by faith in the son of God who loved me and gave himself to die for me" (Galatians 2:20 NIV).

The energy for life comes from Jesus. He is the vine, and we are the branches. The vine supplies the branches with all that is needed to thrive. Without that critical connection, the branch dies. Jesus said that apart from him, we could do nothing (John 15:5 NIV).

Long after my BB gun days, I was a football player in high school. The intense practice sessions would dehydrate my body. When I came home for supper, my mother would serve me tea in a quart jar. I was so thirsty that I drank the first jar quickly and started on my second jar. The tea was refreshing, and my dehydrated body needed the nourishment that the tea had to offer. As I watched the tea stain the water, in Jim's example, I thought of how that tea my mother served hit the spot and relieved my thirst.

Do you hunger and thirst for righteousness? Jesus promised you would be filled (Matthew 5:6 NIV). You have to do it his way by allowing him to come inside to be the agent of change. Do more by allowing less from self, surrendering control to God's Spirit, and enjoying the freedom that He provides.

EPILOGUE

Our journey began when a Texas mama expressed her faith by answering a call to prayer at the Oak Hills Church. Her prayer of faith rose to heaven, and her tears fell to the church house floor. Those tears inspired the title of this book. Those tears are mingled with the tears of all the saints of God as they cry out in times of suffering, shame, and grief. All those prayers await the saints in heaven, where there will be no more tears.

As this book was being written, I shared some of the early chapters with my sister Jane. For twenty-two years, she has fought the crippling disease of MS. To put it simply, she has a PhD in suffering. Her insights are treasured since most of the tears that fall to the church house floor are a result of our sufferings. Her response to those early chapters was simply, "This is sad, Dan." My challenge was clearly to write a book about tears without a lingering sense of sadness, and I hope that message is conveyed. Please notice that in all twelve chapters, God shows up. Most times I have found that you cannot see what God is doing until you see what God has done. No matter what, though, your tears matter to God. You may feel as if you shed them alone, but you did not. God was there with you, though unseen.

There are also tears of joy that fall to the church house floor. We may feel that they are few and far between when compared to the tears of sadness, but I hope we can all cherish those moments even if they are the minority.

We can focus on our tears, but what about the tears of a lonely God? Might it be possible that most of the tears on the church house floor came from a God who aches for us to open up to him? As Jesus entered Jerusalem to suffer the shame and pain of the cross, he cried out, "O Jerusalem, Jerusalem, you who kill the prophets and stone those sent to you, how often I have longed to gather your children together, as a hen gathers her chicks under her wings, but you were not willing" (Matthew 23:37). Those words were spoken over two thousand years ago, and nothing about the heart of God has changed; He still longs for the eyes of your heart to turn to him.

Our journey from the duplex on Fifth Avenue to a blue-sky day at Wrigley Field spans fifty years. It was a deeply personal story for my family. We share it with you not to draw attention to ourselves, nor to resurrect stories of sadness in your life. We share it in hopes that at some point, others might lift their heads heavenward and ask, "God, are you really in this sadness with me? Could it be possible there is a rest of the story for me?" Trust in Him, and allow God to show you the rest of your story.

114

Printed in the United States
By Bookmasters